WHAT THEY THINK IS NOT MY BUSINESS

How Freeing Yourself of Other's Opinions
Can Enable You to Take Control and
Live Your Ultimate Life

JAIME LAING

First published by Ultimate World Publishing 2021
Copyright © 2021 Jaime Laing

ISBN

Paperback: 978-1-922597-25-0
Ebook: 978-1-922597-26-7

Jaime Laing has asserted her rights under the Copyright, Designs and Patents Act 1988 to be identified as the author of this work. The information in this book is based on the author's experiences and opinions. The publisher specifically disclaims responsibility for any adverse consequences which may result from use of the information contained herein. Permission to use information has been sought by the author. Any breaches will be rectified in further editions of the book.

All rights reserved. No part of this publication may be reproduced, stored in or introduced into a retrieval system, or transmitted in any form, or by any means (electronic, mechanical, photocopying, recording or otherwise) without the prior written permission of the author. Any person who does any unauthorised act in relation to this publication may be liable to criminal prosecution and civil claims for damages. Enquiries should be made through the publisher.

Cover design: Ultimate World Publishing
Layout and typesetting: Ultimate World Publishing
Editor: Martine Julie

Ultimate World Publishing
Diamond Creek,
Victoria Australia 3089
www.writeabook.com.au

Testimonials

I've been inspired by Jaime's tenacity since our very first conversation. There are just some people you can hear who have that burning desire within them to succeed no matter what. Working alongside Jaime for the past couple of years, I've been amazed, on so many occasions, as to how she's created outstanding business success despite the obstacles thrown at her and how she's been able to lead and empower an incredible team on a global scale.

Jaime shows up every single day with a Boss Babe mindset and driving force that naturally motivates those around her and pushes them to raise their game too. Throughout my whole career, she's been one of my most favourite people to work with."

~ Kirsty Mailer, Find Your Super Tribe

"I have known Jaime since childhood and whilst life has taken us on our own journeys, it is no surprise to me that Jaime is an exceptional entrepreneur and mentor, inspiring and expanding others to be their best selves in life and business.

Jaime has always been a dedicated, committed and motivational person. Being in her presence, you are engulfed in her passion and enthusiasm for life. Her knowledge of self and how to embody the best version of her, beyond her own self sabotaging ways and limiting beliefs, is without doubt one of her super powers. Her dedication to her own personal development over her lifetime is an absolute honour to her and her commitment to always raising the bar.

Jaime is simply a powerhouse of a woman. When fear strikes, she rises higher, without anyone or herself holding her back. Super proud to know her and inspired to continue watching her shine her light in this world."

~ Sherie Abela, Soul Empowerment Coach

"The foundation to our lifelong friendship started through our love of health and fitness. What I love is that Jaime is someone that shows her true heart and passion, and through her sheer determination, inspires many.

She has developed and nurtures a strong mindset that has created so many successes throughout her 20-year career. It's wonderful how she shows empathy and grace in all she does, which is sometimes lacking in many other entrepreneurs.

Jaime's accomplishments span many, but I've personally witnessed various small business wins, her building inspiring young leaders through her martial arts business, mentoring gym owners to higher levels of personal and business success and more recently engaging in global opportunities. This has expanded her skills and her mindset, and she has proven repeatedly that her ability is endless.

Where her focus goes, energy flows ....and living her dream follows."

~ **Karen Gray**

"Jaime Laing is a young woman embodying her soul mission of personal growth and development. I have worked closely with her over the past 2.5 years and have witnessed someone with a zest for life and a 'can do' attitude who is determined to live to her full potential. She is a calm, pragmatic and intelligent person whose natural flair and qualities as a coach and leader are coupled with a sincere respect for humanity. Her humility, kindness and thoughtfulness enhance her natural authority as a leader and she tells her story here, in the hope it will guide others along their own journey of self-discovery."

~ **Nicola McNamara, Lifestyle Portability**

"My Personal Development journey started a couple of years ago which is around the time I met Jaime Laing. She has become one of my closest friends. Her in-depth knowledge, experience and understanding of Personal Development principles and how they can positively impact our lives, has helped me in my own journey of Personal Growth. Jaime's wholehearted approach to life is evident in her mentoring and coaching and I am grateful to call her my friend."

~ Alison Hillis, Inspired Balance Life

Dedication

To my husband, soul mate, life partner, and best friend, Kevin. If only I could see myself the way you see me. This book was born because of your belief in me and what I had to say.

To my beautiful girls, Brooklyn and Indiana. You are my driving force, my motivation to be better than I was yesterday and to be a demonstration of what it takes to live your absolute best life. No words can explain how much I love you both. Grow up to be the powerhouse women I know you can become.

And to the little girl who dreamed big and believed she could someday be something, this is for you.

Contents

Introduction	1
Chapter 1: You Get To Choose	5
Chapter 2: Ignite Your Fire	19
Chapter 3: Beyond The Box	33
Chapter 4: Master Your Mind	45
Chapter 5: The Decided Heart	65
Chapter 6: Guts, Grit & Staying The Course	77
Chapter 7: The Secret to Sure-Fire Success	93
Chapter 8: Sizzling Synchronicities	107
Chapter 9: Fast Track Your Success	119
Chapter 10: Your Ultimate Arsenal	133
Chapter 11: Power Up Your Results	149
Chapter 12: Effective Kickass Action	159
Afterword	175
Resources	177
About the Author	178
Acknowledgements	181
Testimonials	iii, 183
Bonuses	187-191

Introduction

*The day you **stop caring what other people think** of you is the day your life begins."*
~ Aaron Eckhart

Fear of being judged and, therefore, disliked can stop you in your tracks from doing anything that isn't deemed acceptable. This fear can come from judgement from people directly around us, and from people afar that we don't even know. My earliest memory of being judged as 'different' happened when I was in the fourth grade. I had just changed schools for the second time and was asked "Where's your dad?" by another fourth grader. "I don't have a dad" was my reply. I can still remember the feeling I got from the look on that kid's face. As an adult, I imagine the kid probably had no idea what to say, or what not having a dad even meant, but as the child receiving the look, I felt ashamed, judged and feared of not being accepted.

This fear stayed with me for another thirty years. As did the behaviour of caring about what other people think. I wonder

WHAT THEY THINK IS NOT MY BUSINESS

how different my life would have been if I didn't worry so much about what other people think and realised what other people think is not my business.

Can you relate? Are you thinking, *Yes! I'm sick of fearing what other people think!* You're in the right place. This book will walk you through the steps to break free of other people's judgements and live your life on your terms. It is my hope that I can pass on what I have learnt in my own journey, to assist you to take your life to the next level. I wish I had learnt this when I was ten but better late than never, right?

Changing your life begins the day you stop being concerned with what others think. No matter what you do, people will judge and have an opinion. If you do what is the recommended and acceptable thing, they will judge you for not thinking for yourself. If you do what is outside the box, they will judge you for not doing what is normal or acceptable. To put it nicely, you're between a rock and a hard place when it comes to trying to please others. You're going to be judged either way, so why not be judged on living your best life?

I'll be honest, there are no ground-breaking personal development principles explained here that have not been around for thousands of years. These principles have been studied by theologists, psychologists and philosophers and you may recognise some of them, if not all of them. My hope is that the lessons I have learnt in my journey are of help to you in yours. It may be a simple reminder of something you already know, or a gentle nudge of what you need to do to create better results in your life. Perhaps, you may learn something new that can completely shift where you're currently at. That's why you're here, right? To create a better life for yourself?

INTRODUCTION

Before we begin our journey together, I want you to know that you are not alone. The journey of self-actualisation and discovery can feel like a lonely one, but you are not walking this path by yourself. Having said that, there is only **one** person who can change and create the life you visualise for yourself. YOU. It is solely your responsibility to live your best life, regardless of what other people think.

The truth is, any one of us can create *anything* we truly want. No matter where you are starting from, that life you see for yourself can be your reality. The fear of what others think may always be present, but you will be in control of how much power it has over you. Despite letting go of what other people think, I had to overcome the fear of judgement in writing this book! I still find myself slipping back into the people pleaser I used to be, but with the tools outlined in the following pages, I am able to get back on track and live my life, my way.

Your journey will be individual to you. And just know your journey is the journey you are meant to go on. You are unique, you are amazing and you are meant to shine bright in this life. No one has the right to dull your light. You get to choose how you live your life, for what anyone else thinks is not your business.

Life is just beginning for you.

This is your moment.

To your success,

Jaime Laing

CHAPTER 1

You Get To Choose

It's 1988. Here sits a typical 10-year-old girl. Playing with Barbie dolls and dreaming of being anything she wants on any given day. One day, it is a veterinarian, other days it is a hairdresser and today, it is a 'rich person'. In her mind, there are no limitations. She can be whatever she wants to be. She doesn't see herself as different from any other 10-year-old girl and she gives anything a try. Life is fun and she is happy.

Then slowly, over time, things start to change. Her vision begins to narrow, she starts looking at the people directly around her as to what is possible. She realises that she is indeed different - coming from a single parent family (in the 80s, this was not the norm) and being on the "chubby" side. She starts to understand that money is something that is hard to come by and when you have it, you hold on to it extremely tightly. She also learns that you must work really hard to acquire anything and that sometimes, even after hard work, you never get what you want. In other words, life is a struggle.

WHAT THEY THINK IS NOT MY BUSINESS

A few comments here and there from thoughtless kids and she begins to become extremely body conscious. Trying to fit in, she avoids anything that will make her stand out more. It becomes more of a survival game than an adventure game. Add in changing schools during the formative pre-teen years, she dims her light and does what she has to, to be liked. Over the years, she becomes afraid of stepping outside of the acceptable circle and her voice is dampened.

Seeking acceptance and the need to be liked becomes her new normal. Perhaps because of the biological father who left her as a baby, or because of the perceived difference between her and the other kids at school. It is a huge weight on her shoulders that she will carry through to adulthood. Finally, as she nears the start of her fourth decade, she can no longer live this way. That light begins to get brighter, her voice begins to get louder and she steps into her truth, into her true self, and begins to see the world as it really is - with limitless potential.

That little girl was me.

How deeply I want to take her into my arms and tell her she's amazing and beautiful just as she is and in fact, life IS an adventure and one she should be having fun with. How the only person she should be seeking approval and love from is herself and how she can BE, DO and HAVE anything she wants in life. How both her biological father, and the man she loved as her father, leaving had nothing to do with her and how she is more than deserving of unconditional love. How she doesn't have to be anyone else other than herself. And how she is going to be a kickass, powerhouse, strong boss babe with the world at her feet! How I wish I could hold that little girl and tell her everything I now know.

YOU GET TO CHOOSE

When do we stop believing that anything is possible, that life is amazing and that the opportunities are endless? When do we stop dreaming big? When does it become about what others think more than what we think of ourselves and our lives? When do we stop pursuing our own purpose and soul desires just to please others or to stay in what is perceived as the 'norm'? When do we learn that we, in fact, get to choose how we want to live?

This is your life and you only get one shot at it. Time is the one thing we can never get back and it is your time now to live your life, your way. As I neared turning 40, I had those sorts of questions running through my mind and they became louder and louder until I could no longer ignore them. Whilst I have made some bold decisions in my 20s and 30s, I was also heavily caught up with pleasing others and caring too much about what they thought. It wasn't one or two people that I was worried about, it was anyone really. I am in awe that it took me almost 40 years to get to the point of questioning why I was so bothered by what others thought. Now, I'm not talking about being selfish or conceited, with no concern for others. I'm talking about the direction of your life being driven by what others think you should do rather than what you truly want for yourself.

> *"Opinions are like buttholes. Everyone has one and most of them stink."*
> **~ Unknown**

No matter what you do, when you're trying to please someone, you end up pleasing no one. The people that are so heavily opinionated about what you do in your life are just so incredibly unhappy in their life that they feel the need to put you down, in order to make themselves feel better. Ironic, right? And also freeing. Once you get this, and no longer worry about what others are going to say or think, you become liberated to step into your own power. When you continue to be affected by others, you remain unchanged and at the mercy of outside influences.

What drives the decisions and direction of our lives? Sure, when we are young adults, we listen to those closest to us, while thinking we are making decisions about what we want. I certainly felt that way. Doing the acceptable and expected thing of going to university, finishing the degree, getting the "secure" job, marrying my childhood sweetheart and settling down. Within a few years, I recognised this reality was not my dream reality. By the age of 21, I was working in management and realised being an "employee" specifically was not going to get me where I wanted to be. I knew I had to be a business owner if I was going to create any level of success. Where these thoughts or vision came from, I have no idea. No one in my family had been an entrepreneur, or had accomplished what I wanted. Who was I to think I could break the cycle and be something different? I was just a girl from a broken home who grew up in Western Sydney - how could I possibly have anything more than what I saw around me?

Except, somehow, I believed I could.

And you can too.

Seeing Past the Fog

My first year in university was a long commute from home. Lectures started early which meant leaving home before sunrise most days. There was a stretch of road I needed to drive along that was renowned for heavy fog early in the morning. It was so heavy that you could barely see the road directly in front of the headlights of the car. Could you imagine if I just stopped suddenly because I couldn't see what was in front of me? It would most definitely have ended catastrophically. The key was to not stop, keep moving forward, and sure enough, the fog lifted and the road ahead was clear.

Similarly, in our lives, over time without noticing, a fog can slowly engulf us to the point where we cannot see through it. We may only be able to see what is directly in front of, and around us, not knowing that anything different or better is possible. We continue to do what has always been done. This fog can be formed from limitations imposed upon us through the opinions of others, following other's footsteps and by neglecting to expose what is past the fog. Being able to recognise the fog and choosing to see through it, to what is truly possible, is key to breaking free of the past. What has happened up to this point has no weight on what can happen in the future - but first the fog needs to lift! The road is clear only a few feet in front of you with the fog around you, however beyond that, the road is infinite and endless. How do you move the fog? Action. Forward movement. Changing where you are.

> *"It doesn't matter where you are coming from; all that matters is where you are going."*
> **~ Brian Tracy**

WHAT THEY THINK IS NOT MY BUSINESS

No matter where you have started, you get to choose from this point on. No matter what has happened in your past, you get to choose how you're going to live, and how you're going to change your life.

ACTION

How have you allowed others to affect your decisions or life path? How have you given others power or strength over the choices you have made up to this point?

I can hear some of you already saying, "There's no way I can get past what's happened in my life. It's too big/painful/still present. I've tried before and failed." The very fact that you are reading this tells me otherwise. In fact, you wouldn't have even had the beginning of an idea that life can be different for you *if* you couldn't achieve that. Every successful person out there has become so BECAUSE of adversities. Take Oprah Winfrey. Surviving a traumatic and abusive childhood, Oprah went on to become one of the wealthiest and highly respected women in history. The difference is what you do *because* of your past, and not allowing it to be the reason you do nothing. Age has nothing to do with your options to change your life. At any point, at any age, you get to choose. Colonel Sanders, at 69 years of age, didn't retire. Instead, with a goal of franchising his fried chicken recipe, he went from restaurant to restaurant pursuing his dream. At 88, Colonel Sanders was a billionaire.

The past does not equal the future. Your past has already been written while the future remains unknown. You can choose to take control of your future and create different results no matter what has happened.

YOU GET TO CHOOSE

"I've come to believe that all my past failures and frustrations were actually laying the foundation for the understandings that have created the new level of living I now enjoy."
~ Tony Robbins

Continuing to hold onto things of the past leads you to staying exactly there. In the past. You will not be in control if you remain at the mercy of others, or your previous perceived failures. It's time to take the "horse by the reins", it's time to take back your life and it's time to live your life, your way. Regardless of what others think. That is not your business. Whether you want to change your career or profession, move homes, lose weight, get fitter, find your soul mate, leave a relationship that no longer serves you, create unbelievable wealth, give more or start a charity - you CAN do it. The power within you is far stronger than you can imagine. You just need to tap into it. The first step is in letting go of the past.

"Do not give your past the power to define your future."
~ Unknown

Releasing the Past

The longer we hold onto something, the longer we remain at its effect. The greater the hold it has on us, the more time will pass that you are not in control. Holding onto the past keeps us in the passenger seat, rather than driving our own life. It keeps the shackles on our ankles and stops us from living freely, living how we want to today. What could your life look like in six to twelve months if you let that go?

There are many techniques available to release the past. Some include journaling, writing letters to people who have done wrong by you, visualisation or in extreme circumstances, physically removing yourself from situations. Whatever you choose, do so with velocity and determination. Stick with your decision. This is especially critical when the person or circumstance remains with you. There will be push back, opinions will be flying and it may even get feisty as you take back control of your life. The people who truly love you will stick by you and support you. This is your life. Who are you living it for? Them or you?

Journaling

Journaling is such a powerfully creative technique to tap into the mind. It allows the mind to expand and activates the right side of the brain for creativity and imagination. When using this practice for releasing the past, give yourself permission to pour your heart and soul down onto paper. The act of getting it out of your head and onto paper frees you from the control this person or event has on you. Journaling is also a GREAT method to use to forgive yourself for your responsibility in an event that you are wanting to release. [Yes, there are elements where you are responsible for what has happened!]. Grant yourself the space to be honest, open and as descriptive as possible. The more you get out, the better. Remove the hold it has on you, release it from your life as you draw an end to your journal and close the book.

Write a Letter

I have used this powerful technique many times over the years to rid myself of negative people, feelings or situations and to achieve clarity on what I want. Whether you decide to send the letter or

YOU GET TO CHOOSE

not is up to you, and the situation. It actually doesn't matter if you send it or not, the objective and result will be the same. To rid yourself of the hold the past has on you.

This technique gives you an opportunity to be completely honest and vulnerable, without fear of confrontation. Tell this person exactly what you are feeling and thinking, how you perceive the situation and what you want to happen. Tell them how they made you feel, your truth of the matter, and how this relationship has impacted you. You can take back control of the situation and clear yourself of the negative energy and the hold it has on you. The person also doesn't necessarily need to be alive or still in your life for you to get the full benefit of this technique. The impact this has on your energy and mindset is so powerful regardless.

What you do with the letter once finished can vary from situation to situation. You may very well send it to the person if you want them to know how you feel, or if you want to hear their reply. If this is the case, be prepared for what may be backlash. As you regain control, there may be push back from those who have had the perceived control. If it is a relationship you want to continue, send love to the person while remaining firm in your stand and your boundaries. You are setting the tone for the relationship to move forward and if the person truly loves and respects you, they will respect your feelings.

You may also send your letter to the person without putting their address on the envelope! The action of putting it in the mailbox may be enough of a release for you. You may burn the letter, liberating you or you can even "park" that person or event in a box on a shelf - and leave it there.

Visualising Cutting the Connection

Imagine this with your eyes closed. There is a rope connecting you to something that no longer serves you. As you visualise this rope, what does it look like? Is it thick and heavy or light and thin? Is it frayed and tatty or is it like new? Is it taut or loose? Where is it attached to you? What is it attached to?

Now as you see the rope, imagine cutting through it, breaking the connection between you and the person/event. As you do this, feel the freedom and liberation that comes from it no longer being attached to you. You are free! Enjoy the feelings that come up from this method before opening your eyes and starting your life released from the connection.

Physically Removing Yourself

In some occasions, there may be no other option than to physically remove yourself from a person or situation. There is nothing wrong with acknowledging that being around someone or something just does not serve you. You can love someone from afar, or you can choose to end a relationship. Either is ok if that is what it takes for you to live your best life. You owe it to yourself to be happy and to create a life of your dreams, and sometimes there are people who just cannot accept someone else's happiness. That is on them, not you. Their happiness is their responsibility, not yours.

This may even extend to your job environment or social circle. You may love your job, but the environment is toxic. You may have a social group but the people are not your type of people anymore. Ask yourself, what are the long term effects on my energy and life if I remain in this environment? In most cases, there is no price to your overall happiness and mindset, and removing yourself physically is the only answer. If it is time to move on, just know there is something amazing waiting for you.

ACTION

Decide today to let go of your past. Using one or all of the techniques above, release your past from your today. You get to choose what you hold on to, and what to let go of. Ask yourself, does it serve me to keep this person or situation in my life? Will releasing this free me to live my best life moving forward?

Change Your Focus

"The only time you should look back in life, is to see how far you've come."
~ Kevin Hart

What you focus on ultimately affects your thoughts, feelings, emotions and behaviour. What do you focus on the most? What has happened already, or what is yet to come? Put the focus on what you want, where you are going and onto your future. Through self-fulfilling prophecies, you get more of what you focus on.

WHAT THEY THINK IS NOT MY BUSINESS

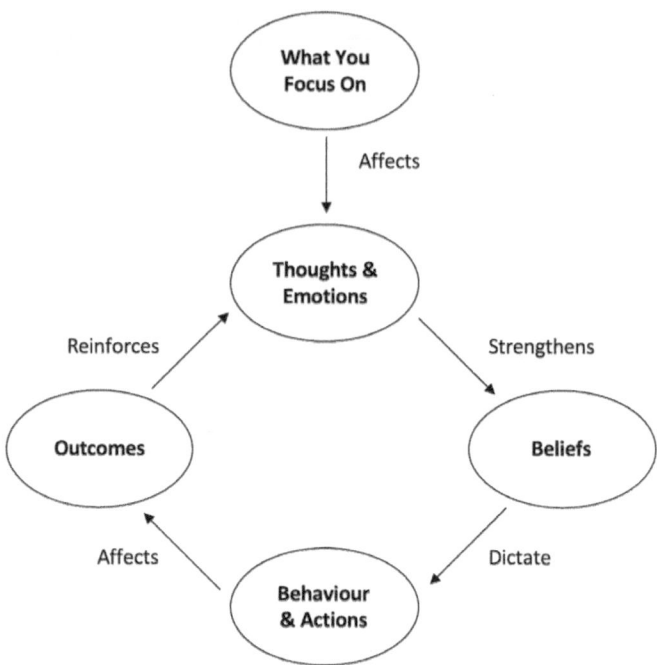

Self-fulfilling prophecies are simply predictions that cause themselves to be true, therefore strengthened, which then only causes more of the same 'prediction'. In the example above, regardless of the positive or negative focus, you get more of what you focus on. Focus on the past - you will get more of the past (through similar events or people coming into your life) and conversely, focus on the future and you get more of what you desire (through events or people coming into your life).

What if you don't know exactly what you want or how to get what you want? First of all, decide you want a change. We get to discover what we truly desire in the next chapter but if you don't know what you want right now, simply decide that you want a change from this point. Don't know how to get what you want? That's ok as well! I had no idea how I was going to become an entrepreneur in my early 20s, I just knew I wanted to be one.

YOU GET TO CHOOSE

Start by deciding you want to change your life, regardless of what others think. Every change begins with a decision. Every waking moment, focus on the possibility of a new life. Only look back to see how far you've come. The more you remain focused on the direction you want to go, the more you will attract circumstances and people to support movement in that direction.

Be Open to Opportunities

This is the exciting part! Be open to new opportunities presenting themselves! By opening yourself to possibilities, you open your heart to new beginnings and new ways of thinking. I had no idea the business I am in now would be the business that would take me to where I wanted to go. In fact, being open allowed me to answer a little Facebook advertisement to enquire about a business that ten years before I would never have even considered. My past experiences got me to where I was, but if I had remained closed off to opportunities such as this, I would have missed the chance to change my life and create the success I have achieved. The same goes with love. By being open to finding my soul mate, he appeared - and actually had been there for seven years before I "saw" him as that.

Chances are, the path to creating what you want will not be the path that you think will take you there. It took me a while to grasp this. After many years of frustration and wondering, "Why hasn't this happened?!" I finally let go of the outcome and a new door opened! Voilà! It can all happen very quickly, if you release the expectation of it happening a certain way and just remain open to the possibility of it manifesting in any way.

What others think about your life, what you want to achieve and the decisions you make, is not your business. You have an opportunity to lift the fog, start at zero, release the past and redesign your life. It's about moving past your current circumstances to create the life you want. Be open to change happening and opportunities, people and events appearing that you could never have imagined. Expect doors to open and be willing to look into them. They will open and when they do, you'll wonder where they have been hiding all this time.

CHAPTER SUMMARY

- You get to choose - at any point, at any age - how to live your life.

- Looking past the fog reveals unlimited possibilities.

- You are not your past, nor does it equal your future.

- Let go of what other people think and live your life, your way. You'll never please everyone anyway, so why try?

- What you focus on, you get more of.

- Be open to opportunities and change happening in ways you wouldn't expect.

Designing your ideal life is where the fun begins in Chapter 2! Ignite a fire deep within you that will cause a blazing desire, making you truly unstoppable in your quest to living a 10/10 life.

CHAPTER 2

Ignite Your Fire

"Vision will ignite the fire of passion that fuels our commitment to do whatever it takes to achieve excellence."
~ Tony Dungy

I spent most of my teenage years and early 20s staying within the invisible boundaries of what I thought at the time was acceptable. I didn't want to upset anyone or be different. I wanted to be loved and accepted. However, when I felt in the pit of my stomach that I wasn't on the right path, I knew there was only one thing to do. Change my circumstances or live a life that was not what I truly wanted.

Change for me meant leaving a marriage that wasn't working, leaving the 'safety' of a salary paying job and becoming an entrepreneur. More recently, I chose an exciting business that is non-traditional, as there was still something in my soul that was telling me there was more out there for me.

Listening to that inner voice or deep feeling takes courage. To stay where it's acceptable or safe keeps you living under an external control. Being bold and admitting to yourself you want a different life takes guts. I want you to know, you've got this. I see you and I hear you. While others may not understand or may criticise you, that's on them. You are taking steps towards your best life and the people that matter most will stick by you.

Wheel of Life

Let's start crafting your dream life! Leave the past in the past. Leave the mechanics or the *how* for later and let's design your ideal life. What area/s of your life are you not 100% happy in? What do you want to change or improve? Let's take a look at each of the areas of your life in our Wheel of Life.

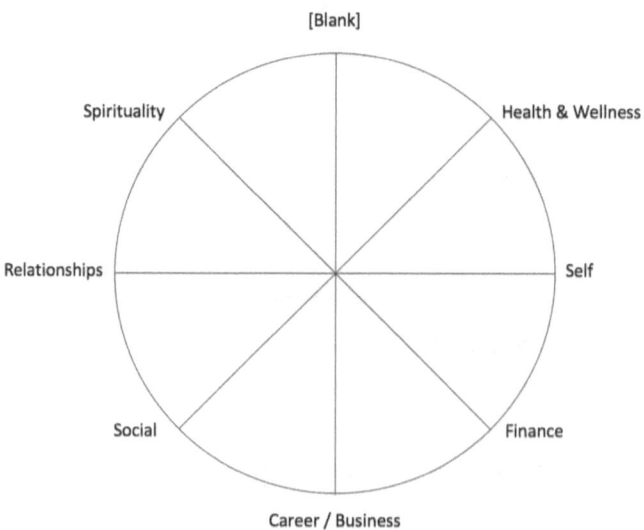

IGNITE YOUR FIRE

Feel free to change any of the segments of your Wheel. I have intentionally left the top one blank for you to add in another important area. You can download a blank template at www.jaimelaing.com/bonus.

Once you have identified all the important areas of your life, rank each area out of ten; rating how satisfied and happy you are in that area. The centre of the wheel is zero and the outside of the wheel is ten. Zero is completely unsatisfied and unhappy, ten is completely satisfied, can't improve it in any way, super pumped and happy. Place a cross and write the number on the line of each area where you currently rank. Once you have ranked each area, join the crosses! Here's an example of what your Wheel may look like:

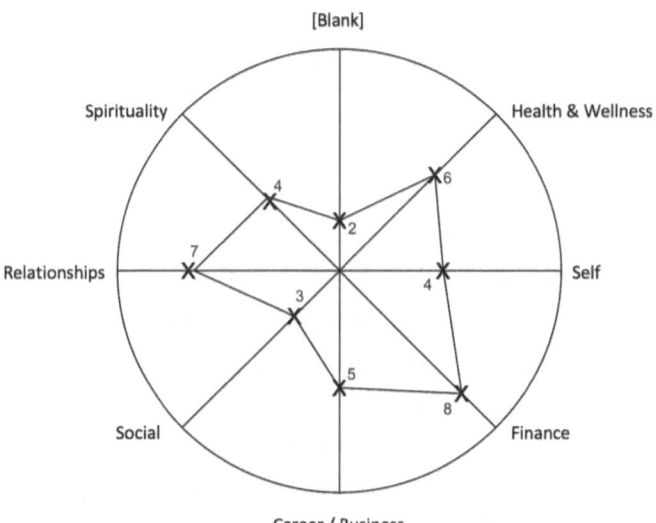

How small or large is your wheel? How far would your wheel go hypothetically if you had to roll it? Is it lopsided or jagged? Ultimately, everyone desires a big round wheel meaning ranking 10/10 for each area. At points throughout your life, this may be the case, at other times not so. This is an exercise you can do anytime to gauge your happiness level in your overall life and highlight any area that you may want to work on.

A 10/10 Life

Here's where it gets fun! For each area, write down what your life would look like if it was 10/10. What would need to be present or absent? Would you need to change anything? The more detail the better. You are crafting your ideal life, so have fun and go for it!

> *"Start embracing the life that is calling you. Find your calling. Know what sparks the light in you, so you - in your own way - can illuminate the world."*
> **~ Oprah Winfrey**

As you design a life that fills your heart with happiness, remove any limitations of what you perceive as "impossible". If you can think it, you can absolutely achieve it, so let the pen flow freely and imagine what your ultimate life would look like. Gaining crystal clear clarity in what you want will put you back in the driver's seat. This is where you *ignite your fire* and become unstoppable! The action of writing your 10/10 life will set in motion a movement and progression towards your vision. It is this fire that will drive you forward, through the rubble, over the hurdles and to the life you want to live.

Turn Your Ember into A Blazing Fire

"The trouble with not having a goal is that you can spend your life running up and down the field and never score."
~ Bill Copeland

Without goals and a vision to work towards, chances are you will fall into someone else's plan. Failing to work towards what YOU want will lead to a life without purpose, without direction and at the affect of others. You will fall into someone else's plan, and guess what they have planned for you? Probably not much. Setting goals and working persistently towards those goals gives you meaning and sets you on the path to a purpose driven life.

Igniting your deepest desires and turning them into a blazing fire begins with discovering your **why**. *Why do you want change? Why are you looking to make a difference? Why do you want to feel, be, or live a certain way?* Finding your why provides you with meaning and drive. When you know what your why is, you have a sense of determination that nothing can shake. Discovering my why began when I was introduced to Life Coaching. Until that point, I wasn't really sure what I wanted to achieve in life. I left school, went to university and got a job - all the 'expected' things. My degree was in the Health and Fitness industry and whilst I enjoyed helping others achieve their fitness goals, I definitely felt like there was more out there for me. I completed a Life Coaching course and not long after that, I left my job, and my first marriage broke down. Despite the tumultuous time, in hindsight I can appreciate that my *why* was driving my actions and behaviour forward. I wasn't living my absolute best life, so I made moves to align myself closer to my why.

WHAT THEY THINK IS NOT MY BUSINESS

Over the years, my why definitely grew stronger. After having my beautiful girls, it deepened even more. I wanted to make a positive difference in people's lives, all round. I wanted to assist others to live their best life, step into their best selves and break the chains of what was holding them back. I have a deep belief that anyone can achieve anything they want, if they only BELIEVE it, and ACT on it. I wanted to be the person to bridge the gap between someone's goal and their disbelief in the achievement of that goal. Nothing gives me more satisfaction or joy than seeing someone transform their life and create what was unimaginable prior to that point. I had experienced someone believe in me like this and I wanted to be that person for others. Discovering my why opened my eyes to how I wanted to live and what I wanted to do with my life. Simon Sinek et al explain in Finding Your Why:

> "Once you know your WHY, you have a choice to live it every day. Living it means consistently taking actions that are in alignment with the things you say...When the things we say and the things we do are aligned with what we believe, we are fully living our WHY."

ACTION

Take some time and go through your 10/10 life. Why do you want to create the changes you have listed? Here are some questions to help get to the heart of your why.
- What is it about this 10/10 life that is driving you?
- What are the underlying desires? Who do you want to Be? Why do you want to be Doing what you have written? Why do you want to Have what you desire?

IGNITE YOUR FIRE

- Who will be affected or influenced by you living this life?
- What are the feelings you are searching for in living this way?
- Who are you around when you are most fulfilled and satisfied?
- How are you contributing when you feel fulfilled and on purpose?

There are no right or wrong answers here. Be completely honest with yourself. Forget other's expectations or desires. This is about you and what sets your heart on fire. Discovering your why will renew your passion and give you a sense of direction. Understanding your why will offer you a new lens through which to look at your life.

My why is being of service to others, specifically in assisting them to live their best life - irrespective of their history or what others think. When I became a mum, my why deepened as I wanted to, first of all, be a demonstration to my girls but, secondly, to give them the space to live their absolute best life without restrictions, judgements or limitations. Once you have discovered your 10/10 life, putting meaning behind it will strengthen it ten fold. The stronger the reason, the stronger the why, and the stronger the drive to achieve it.

The more descriptive you can be about your fire and your why, the better. This is crucial to ensuring you are aiming for exactly what you want. For me, when I was discovering my why, it wasn't enough to simply write down to be of service to others. This has so many meanings! Instead, by getting crystal clear on *what* being of service meant for me, ensured I attracted the right opportunity into my life. I want to assist others in living their best life, overcoming self-limiting beliefs, being a bridge between where they are and where they want to go, so working with other like-minded, goal oriented, driven people who want a better life for themselves is my fire. The more you can detail what you want and why, the better. It's no surprise then that the business I find myself in today is in the area of assisting others to create their dream life!

When uncovering your why, your purpose and what sets your heart on fire, you may find limitations creeping in.

> *I can't do this because...*
> *This person will say that...*
> *That's not possible because...*
> *That's nice but not realistic...*

While you keep the restrictions alive, you're right in that it will be impossible for your fire to be lit. Inside each of you is that little girl or boy who believed anything was possible. This is about connecting to your soul and discovering your deepest desires...in spite of what others think or any imposed limitations. Allow yourself space to open your heart, remove any limitations, replace them with positive words and discover your fire.

Where Attention Goes, Energy Flows & Results Show

What do you think about most? When you find yourself daydreaming, are you thinking about the challenges surrounding you, the feeling of being stuck in your circumstances or that conversation you had with someone who left you feeling flat and down? Or are you thinking of the possibilities of the next chapter, the excitement of what the future holds and the anticipation of your desires coming into your life? Listen to the words you speak to others. Do you whinge, complain and bitch over things that have already happened and about other people? Or do you speak positively and enthusiastically about the people, possibilities and opportunities around you? Hear what you are saying to yourself. Do you criticise and judge yourself, thinking things you would never say to anyone else? Or do you internally uplift yourself with love and encouragement, being your biggest cheerleader? Whatever your answer is, is what you'll get more of in life.

Where your attention goes, energy flows. Emily Maroutian explains this well:

> "Energy is the currency of The Universe. When you 'pay' attention to something, you buy that experience. So, when you allow your consciousness to focus on someone or something that annoys you, you feed it your energy, and it reciprocates the experience of being annoyed."

The same flow of energy occurs with positive thoughts. When you focus on the good, you feed it your energy and you draw positive experiences, people and events into your life.

ACTION

Self-check time. It wasn't until this was pointed out to me that I realised what I was saying and therefore attracting! Are your words and thoughts in alignment with what you desire? With your why? Be brutally honest with yourself, because it all starts from here. This is about what you focus on predominantly being what you will get more of. This is a proven self-fulfilling prophecy, either negatively or positively.

WHAT THEY THINK IS NOT MY BUSINESS

Take the time to listen to those around you also. Chances are you will be surprised at what is being said. It's not about judging others. It is about taking control of your position in your life. When you are aware of what you (and others) focus on through language and communication, you will be able to see the flow of energy and the results that come from that. You then have a choice of what you want to put your attention on, and with whom you want to surround yourself. Don't underestimate the power of someone else's words affecting your energy flow either. Inadvertently, this energy can flow into your life - and support you in your journey, or slow you with negativity and pessimism. This can be a hard realisation, and ultimately the decision of living your best life or falling into someone's else's plan will be yours.

Nurturing Your Flame

Igniting your flame and nurturing it must be your priority as, if left unattended, the flame will go out. Not everyone will support your goal, and that's totally fine. They're not you, nor are they living your life. What they think is not your business. The only person that needs to believe in your goals is you. Do you truly believe you can achieve this vision? Without 100% belief, it will remain a hope. I believe you can create exactly what you have written above, because if it wasn't possible for you, it would never have even entered your consciousness as an option. If you can think it, you can create it.

For some, your flame may have just been lit. For others, you may have a long-burning ember that you haven't known how to turn into a blazing fire. No matter where you are, we will work through tools to move you towards your ideal reality. Your actions must be in alignment with your vision. If you are wanting to lose those extra kilos, but you are eating more than you need, obviously you won't budge the scales. If you are wanting to meet your soul mate but are not putting yourself out there, obviously you won't meet anyone. If you're wanting to become an entrepreneur but haven't explored any opportunities, then you will remain at the mercy of a J.O.B (Just Over Broke!) Self sabotage is so powerful *until* you recognise it. Once you have called it for what it is, you move into the driver's seat and get back in control of the destination.

Finding Your Inspiration or Mentor

I mentioned that my entrepreneurial spark was lit early in my career. I was 21 when I met Jon Mailer who, to me at the time, was super successful in running his own business. Jon exuded happiness and charisma, he was making a difference in other people's lives, plus his lifestyle matched his success - driving a luxury car, living in an exotic location, and having the freedom to travel and spend time with his family. He had overcome some pretty big obstacles in reaching that level of success and he truly inspired me to reach new levels, both personally and professionally. The impact Jon had on me, to this day, has changed how I view my life. I believed I too could be an entrepreneur and live an incredibly great life changing people's lives. My goal posts moved and the bar was raised in what I wanted to create. I was no longer happy with being an employee or making someone else rich, nor was I content in devoting eight to nine hours per day to someone else's success. I wanted that for myself. I lost contact with Jon over the years but the effect he has on my flame is permanent.

My desire grew by the day and the fire continued to burn brighter. Having known someone who has done what I wanted to do was one of the driving forces for me during tough moments. Of course,

WHAT THEY THINK IS NOT MY BUSINESS

the road is never straight to success so having someone to look to - even from a distance - can keep you going. You don't necessarily need to personally know someone for them to have that kind of effect on you. You don't even have to want the same "type" of goal for their achievement to impact your belief in it happening for you. If your fire is bright enough, if your why is strong enough and if you deepen your belief with evidence of other's success, anything is possible.

We live in a world of so much opportunity that achieving most of the goals you have for your future are almost certain. In the beginning, you'll have to simply believe in yourself when there is nothing and no one to see you through but the *fire in your belly*.

CHAPTER SUMMARY

- Using the Wheel of Life, rank your current level of happiness out of ten. What needs to happen or change for you to live a 10/10 life?

- Discovering your why will strengthen and deepen your determination to live your 10/10 life.

- Where attention goes, energy flows and results show. Be a magnet by ensuring you are speaking and thinking in alignment with what you desire.

- Success leaves clues. Be inspired by other people achieving what you want or living the life you desire. There is someone who is already doing what you want to do. Creating a strong belief system that it is possible will give you the extra confidence in yourself.

The only limitations are the ones we impose on ourselves. In Chapter 3, we will discover the imaginary box we live in and how to get out of the comfort zone to where life really begins!

CHAPTER 3

Beyond The Box

"If nothing changes, nothing changes."
~ Unknown

Staying safe and at ease inside your comfort zone feels like a big warm hug from your mum when you were a kid. Nothing can harm you, and you feel protected. Except what you truly want is on the *outside* of this zone. Remaining in the cosiness of your comfort zone will just give you bed sores! Doing what you've always done will continue to give you what you've always got. You're here for different results, right? Then it's time to get comfortable being *uncomfortable*. Something has to change for your reality to change.

Growing up, we only know what our parents tell us. We believe with absolute certainty that it is the way they say it is. You may find yourself to this day repeating phrases or reacting in the same way they do or did. As a child, we absorb everything around us at a subconscious level, which is why we sometimes hear our parents' words from our own mouths as adults. We don't know what we don't know, and that is fine when you're a young child dependent on others to guide you. However, as adults we need to take responsibility for our own thoughts and to look beyond the box to know what the truth is for us. What your parents taught you may have been the true for them, but it doesn't mean that it's true for you.

Have you seen horses with blinders on? Blinders (otherwise called blinkers or winkers) are cups made from leather or plastic attached to the bridle that restrict the horse's field of vision. They are used to keep a horse focused and calm. The blinders control where the horse can look, keeping their vision clear forwards and blocking what's going on in the periphery or in the rear. They have no idea of what is happening around them as they can only see what is directly in front of them. Just like a horse with blinders on, we can become closed off to possibilities and opportunities. Looking beyond the box is like removing blinders and seeing what was there the whole time. It is your responsibility to open yourself and discover the boundless potential of this life.

What is the Box?

The box can vary from person to person. The box is simply the restrictions, expectations or beliefs placed on you from other people. Whether that is your parents, your partner, past teachers, friends or colleagues, or on a larger scale media, global or political limitations. The box keeps you playing small and also keeps everyone else happy in themselves. Maybe you were told you have to go to university to get a good job? Or that you must marry young as there's a finite number of people in the world? You could have been told that money doesn't grow on trees (a favourite family saying when I was growing up), or that rich people are selfish who steal from the poor. Whatever limited thinking has been imbedded in your mind has kept you confined in a box. This is not about proving other people wrong but rather simply looking outside the box at what else is possible and what the truth is *for you*. There is someone living the exact life you desire, which I bet is not within the box you find yourself in.

> *"A great many people think they are thinking when they are merely rearranging their prejudices."*
> **~ William James**

There are definite expectations or normal standards placed upon us throughout our life. Some are required to keep society safe, others are to keep you playing small. If what you want is within the box, awesome! Chances are it's not, so it's time to pop our heads up and take a look around. I speak to lots of people on a daily basis, all looking to create different results in their life. When I ask them what income they would like to be earning if there were no limitations, a large number of people will say something along the lines of, "I don't want to be greedy, just enough to get by." How is wanting a better life financially for you and your family being greedy? This is a prime example of being stuck in the box - and it is simply to avoid being judged or looked negatively upon by the rest of the people in the box. Nobody wants to make anyone feel uncomfortable so they will restrict what they truly want to appease others which in turn creates a mediocre life for them. Look outside and see there are so many opportunities to live an extraordinary life.

WHAT THEY THINK IS NOT MY BUSINESS

Looking outside the box is preparing you for your goals to manifest in unexpected ways. If you already knew how to achieve what you want, you would have done it already, right? Your goals will almost always NEVER come about how you expect them to. Becoming an entrepreneur in my early days was about running a bricks and mortar traditional-style business, having a physical location to go to everyday, having staff, stock and "things" to manage. Being 'busy' and working long hours was the way I thought my success would come. I never in a million years imagined myself in an online business that is by definition "outside of the box". I got to a point in my life where I yearned for a better way, I felt there had to be more out there for me. This little thought was like tearing the box apart and seeing for the first time. If I hadn't opened myself to other ways of doing business, regardless of what other people thought, I would still be feeling unfulfilled and stuck.

Looking outside the box doesn't need to be a public announcement! There is no need to declare you won't be confined! In fact, when I went in search for something else outside of my traditional business, I told no one. Not even my husband. He found me watching some video information and asked what I was looking at. I didn't even tell him then instead just replied briefly that I was "looking into something". It wasn't until I learned for myself, did the appropriate research and *decided* in my heart that this was what I wanted to do that I then discussed it with him. Making a statement that you are indeed looking outside the box could give others the opportunity to knock you down before you even get started.

When you can recognise how you have kept yourself in the box, you are then able to remove those blinders, and look beyond your immediate circumstances. When you look outside, you will create the space for a possible new reality.

ACTION

Take a moment to look at the box you are in, or have kept yourself in. Where have you held yourself back with in-the-box thinking? Where have you perhaps held others within the box? How are you limiting yourself and appeasing others? When have you chosen the comfort zone over getting uncomfortable?

More importantly, what can you look at through a different lens to perhaps see new opportunities and possibilities? Brain dump into your journal and begin to tear that box apart.

Get Comfortable Being Uncomfortable

"Life begins at the end of your comfort zone."
~ Neale Donald Walsch

Think about the last time you were in a situation that made you extremely nervous, where you questioned why you had agreed to do something. It may have been getting on a rollercoaster with the kids, speaking in front of a large group of people, or even taking on a temporary role that you felt you weren't exactly ready for. Your heart starts to pound, your hands start to sweat, your thinking goes haywire and your head is in a spin. *"Why, oh why did I agree to this?"* runs through your head on repeat. Then it's over. Your blood pressure returns to normal, the sweating almost instantly stops and you can think clearly again. Except you're asked to do that thing again. *"Why, why again?"* However, this time, the heart isn't beating as fast, the sweating, although still there, doesn't seem so profuse and (dare I say) you're a little excited? You are conditioning your body and stretching your comfort zone each time to a greater level so it gets easier the more you do something. I won't say getting on a big rollercoaster will EVER ease the nerves completely but the nerves are replaced by enjoyment and adrenaline!

The same process occurs when you are going for something outside the box. You question yourself, your heart beats faster, your hands sweat and you may feel fuzzy in the head. Just know that this will pass, you are on the edge of your comfort zone and about to break into the growth zone. The more times you push your boundaries, the more growth you will experience and what was once challenging for you will no longer cause uncontrolled sweating!

I suffer badly from nervous sweating. About ten years ago, I started hosting awards ceremonies for our traditional business with an audience ranging from 120 to 160 people. I can still remember the first awards night. I actually had to carry a handkerchief around with me to keep wiping my hands because I was sweating so badly! How embarrassing. Over the years, the sweating didn't stop completely but it did ease A LOT. I found it easier and easier to get in front of people and even felt comfortable to crack a few jokes! Quite simply, the more I did it, the more confident I became and the easier it got.

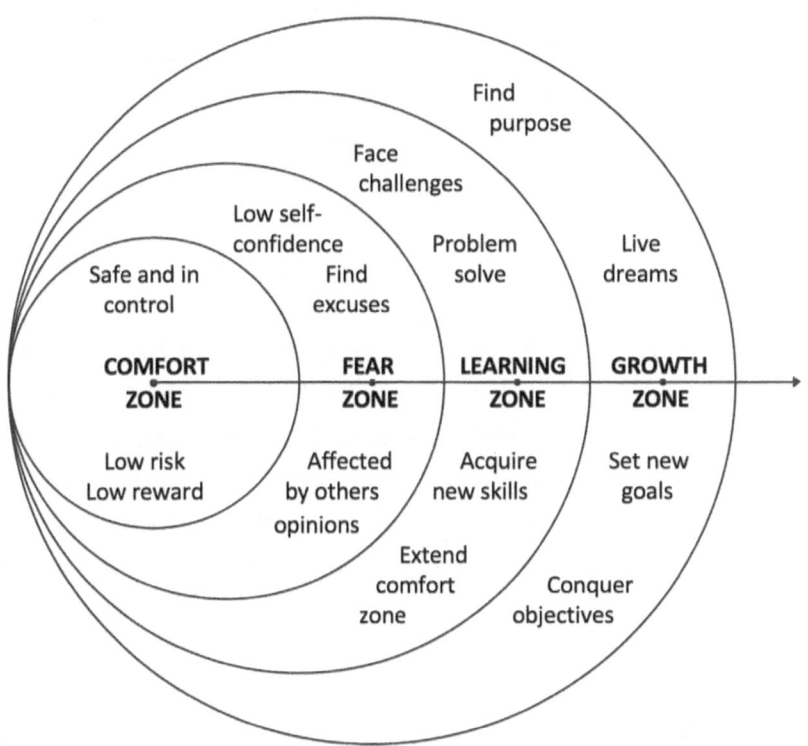

The Comfort Zone

If the prospect of doing something outside of your comfort zone is too much for you, start small. Begin with smaller things that push the boundaries. Maybe getting in front of 160 people makes you do a little wee in your pants (no, that did not happen to me!), so perhaps start with talking in front of two to three friends. If public speaking isn't your thing but you want to reach a larger audience, try using social media as a platform. Whatever you want is on the outside of where you feel safe and comfortable. If you stay in the comfort zone, where there is low risk, and low reward, nothing will change. Taking steps to reach the growth zone (as shown above) will lead to living a life of purpose, conquering objectives, as well as new opportunities and exciting possibilities.

WHAT THEY THINK IS NOT MY BUSINESS

"Getting comfortable with discomfort requires practice, and starting small can be a great way to cultivate the tolerance we all need to keep at it."
~ Dr. Clark

Trust Yourself

There's a reason they're called your goals, that's because they are YOUR goals. What other people think you should do with your life simply is not your business, despite their well intentions. At the end of the day, if the goal lights your fire, if you are pushing your boundaries and growing, trust yourself. Be willing to take a chance, back yourself and take the necessary action to make it a reality. Not everyone will agree with your decision and that is totally ok. It's not their life.

Once you have set your mind on something, go for it. If an opportunity arises which makes your fire burn brighter, be brave and back yourself. Nothing worthwhile was ever achieved by playing small. Believe in yourself and your ability to create the life you deserve. Do you see others creating success from this opportunity? Why couldn't you do it then? Do your due diligence, but don't get paralysis by analysis. If it feels right, if it makes the pit of your stomach ache and if you truly believe you can do it, do it.

"It isn't enough to think outside the box. Thinking is passive. Get used to acting outside the box."
~ Tim Ferriss

BEYOND THE BOX

My in-the-box thinking almost stopped me from starting my online business. I was very sceptical about "those types of businesses". Ironically, my scepticism was not even from my own experiences but from the opinions of others. Totally in-the-box thinking, right? Anyway, I deeply believed there had to be something more out there, but I wasn't sure what that meant. When I went through the information outlining the business model, I was waiting for the confirmation of all the in-the-box thinking I was having. I was running all the limiting beliefs from what other people told me about 'these' businesses. After completing the overview, I realised how wrong I was. If I had let my previous in-the-box thinking dictate my actions, I probably would have never even looked at the information. THIS business was different and was exactly what I wanted. When I decided to get started, I wanted to tell everyone. I thought it was an incredible opportunity and I was ready to share! I wouldn't bring it up first (as it's not my style to talk about myself) but if someone asked me about it, I was off to town! I soon learnt I should keep my cards close to my chest, and for good reason. Not everyone is excited like I am. Not everyone believes in entrepreneurship. Not everyone felt the same way I did. I didn't need anyone's approval or belief in me or my ability to create success. All I needed was to trust myself and back myself. That's all you need as well. Sure, having the support of those closest is important, but trusting your own intuition, decisions and abilities should be paramount.

> *"If someone isn't what others want them to be, the others become angry. Everyone seems to have a clear idea of how other people should lead their lives, but none about his or her own."*
> **~ Paulo Coelho**

WHAT THEY THINK IS NOT MY BUSINESS

Choose who you confide in carefully, as even well-meaning friends and family can dampen your enthusiasm with their own in-the-box-thinking. This may mean keeping your big goals to yourself until you've made progress (or even reached them), it could mean putting in boundaries, or just choosing what to share and what not. I don't think anyone consciously wants to put someone else's dreams or aspirations down but I do think sometimes comments can be made from the other person's lack of knowledge, experience in the area, limited information or arrogance. Until you are confident in being able to not take on anyone else's opinions, keep things close.

ACTION

Recognise potential 'dampeners' to your progress with limited thinking. How can you put steps in place now to guard your growth? (Setting boundaries, minimising contact, choosing your confidantes, etc).

What can you do to strengthen you uncomfortable-ness? What can you do that will push you out of your comfort zone?

CHAPTER SUMMARY

- Staying in your comfort zone using in-the-box thinking will continue to get you the same results you've always gotten.

- Know for yourself with your own research and experience.

- Everything you want is outside of your comfort zone.

- Stretching your comfort zone will give you opportunities to learn new things, expand your horizons, and will get easier the more times you do it.

- Trust yourself, back yourself and choose carefully who you share your dreams with.

We're ramping things up with now being able to see through the limitations that have kept us in the box - by others, by society and even by ourselves. We've got our dream life and vision for ourselves mapped out and we know the past doesn't equal what is possible for us in the future. While learning and developing all of this is essential for our success, it is meaningless if the six inches between our ears isn't aligned with our goals. In Chapter 4, we will discover why mastering your mind is one of the most powerful steps you will take in achieving everything you desire.

CHAPTER 4

Master Your Mind

*"It doesn't matter what happens physically or on the outside, if **your mind is strong and stays in the game.** The second the mind gives up, the body follows."*
~ Ant Middleton, SAS Soldier & Chief Instructor

Your greatest asset - or greatest handicap - is your mind. What goes on in the six inches between your ears can strengthen you and just as easily weaken you. The power of the mind can be used to create the most phenomenal outcomes and drive you to success. However, it also has the power to enslave you and withhold everything you want. Harnessing its power and using it maximally is what separates the best from the rest. It can be your greatest ally or your worst enemy. In fact, simply by shifting gears and mastering your mind, you will awaken to a new life of power and opportunity. Your way of thinking and mindset has gotten you

WHAT THEY THINK IS NOT MY BUSINESS

to where you are today and in order to create a different result and life, you need to change the way you use your mind. Our emotions and behaviours are influenced by even the simplest of thoughts, which can have the greatest of effects.

> *"We cannot solve our problems with the same thinking we used when we created them."*
> **~ Albert Einstein**

Understanding the power of the mind can be both frightening and so damn exciting. To think you are the creator of your life through your thoughts could either immobilise you or empower you. This is not whacky, esoteric gibberish. Rather, it is scientifically proven. Elite athletes understand the power of the mind and ensure they are in peak state both physically and mentally for their competition. How far would a professional athlete get if they trained consistently for years, but didn't really believe in their mind they were capable of winning? Or how do you think their body would *respond* if they pushed themselves to their limit physically but their mind was telling them it's a waste of time? They would NOT win. Nor would they be in a peak state. High performance athletes know they cannot rely on their skill level alone to create success and keep them at the top of their game.

Whilst there are things we cannot control - the weather, other people, economy, traffic, the past - the one thing we have absolute control over is our mind. Learning how to master your mind plants you firmly in the driver's seat and creates an impermeable shield around you. The strength created from understanding and harnessing this power is immeasurable.

MASTER YOUR MIND

"You have power over your mind - not outside events. Realise this, and you will find strength."
~ Marcus Aurelius

In 2007, I was given a movie to watch from a friend. I had heard of it but had no idea what it was about. The movie was "The Secret" based on a book written by Australian author, Rhonda Byrne. I questioned how I had not known about this universal power and principle before. This movie alone unlocked my mind and was my first insight into understanding this powerful resource. In the most basic explanation, the movie explores the Law of Attraction and how to use the power of the mind to attract that which you desire. To me, this discovery was like finding the pot of gold at the end of a rainbow. It was also the catalyst in learning how to master my mind and create everything I've ever wanted.

Learning to harness your mind power is a process and a journey unique to the individual. In mastering your thoughts and mindset, you will clear blockages, past conditioning and self-limiting beliefs. In looking deeper at your mindset in different situations, you will uncover considerations and habits you didn't even realise you had. As you strengthen the mind, others may not know how to take you as you "start to be more positive". You will begin to think differently, speak differently and act differently.

By mastering your mind, you will create an impermeable shield around you. This shield will protect you from the negativity of others' shitty thinking, but don't get me wrong - it will be tested. And also strengthened. What others think is on them, not you. It's not your business to worry or change someone else's thoughts or mindset. Some will be attracted to you more, and not even know why. They will say they just feel happy when they're around you!

WHAT THEY THINK IS NOT MY BUSINESS

What this is, is your energy and vibration. This is where it starts to get exciting!

Understanding the power of the mind is like seeing behind the scenes of a screen play. From the audience's viewpoint, you see the characters acting, the props and the story being played out. However, backstage, there are make-up artists working away, the costume department busily changing the actors, and the director is running around ensuring everyone is where they are meant to be. Without the backstage work going on, the screen play wouldn't be the best performance it can be. The backstage work gives order to the show, direction for the actors and maintains the structure of the script. The same principle applies to the mindset. With a clear, positive, focused mind (the backstage), your life (the screenplay) will play out exactly how you want it to.

> *"Remember that your thoughts are the primary cause of everything."*
> **~ Rhonda Byrne**

What is Mindset?

Your mindset is a series of thoughts and beliefs that shape your perception, attitude and feelings toward something. It is your frame of mind, or way of thinking. It is this collection of thoughts that determine habits. For the most part, a lot of people go through life with minimal attention to what they are thinking and therefore creating in their life.

Have you known someone who has a negative spin to their conversation, no matter what the topic is? They speak of everything they don't want, and they seem to be in a constant battle with life. It is hard and they think everyone is against them. These people are imprisoned by negativity, with every thought creating misery. This mindset in turn is reinforced and confirmed as negative situations and events continue to happen in their life, making them believe with more conviction that life is hard. It doesn't matter what anyone says to these people, they will fight for their negative beliefs. Oh, they are so draining!

Conversely, positive, successful, happy people speak in terms of possibilities, about what they want in their life, and they wholeheartedly believe they can achieve anything they set their mind to. They believe their mind is their ally and they choose what enters their mind carefully, including who they converse with. They are the gatekeeper for their mindset, as they are aware of its incredible power.

Repetitive patterns of thinking - both negative and positive - move from conscious to unconscious thoughts and literally become wired into our brain. This can be explained as acting on auto-pilot. An astonishing 95% of the time, our actions, emotional responses and thoughts are dictated from our unconscious mind. This auto-pilot, or past conditioning runs the show without us even realising it, and is vastly formed by the age of six years old!

ACTION

What is your go-to response when faced with a stressful situation or conflict? Are you on the defensive without taking a moment to assess the situation? Are you a people pleaser, avoiding your true thoughts and going along with others despite not agreeing? Can you effectively evaluate the situation whilst standing your ground without going into flight or fight? What actions (if any) do you take?

These responses are coming from an unconscious level of neurological hardwiring in your brain and more importantly, can be consciously changed by first becoming aware of them.

Where Do Our Mindsets Come From?

The vast majority of our beliefs are formed by our parents, family, teachers, partners, people that come and go from our life, the media, events, past experiences, and knowledge learned. They are formed by us *accepting what is true for us*.

Now, when we were children, we didn't know what we didn't know. We believed our parents when they told us Santa was real and didn't question them when they said, "There's no money for that." In fact, when we are kids, everything we see or hear we take as literal truth. We don't have the ability to question the truth behind what was taught to us and as we grow up, our lens of life broadens, giving us more perspective. We start to learn from our peers, teachers and experiences.

MASTER YOUR MIND

Then, there are moments that happen where we conclude something to be real. Coming from a single parent home, my mum worked long hours and from about ten years of age, I was a "latch-key" kid. I would walk home after school, let myself in and wait for mum to get home a few hours later. Back in those days, mobile phones were non-existent and the phone companies billed for the actual number of phone calls you made for the month. Mum would tell me over and over to not use the phone as she couldn't afford the bill. Sneakily, I would ring a friend or two after school but I would keep a tally of how many calls I would make so that mum didn't notice. As an adult retelling this story to my mum, we can laugh, but as a kid, I developed a deep belief there just wasn't enough to go around. I learned you had to count everything to make sure you didn't blow your budget and to hold onto your money really tight, because there was never enough. How did this belief translate into my adulthood and later into my entrepreneurial journey? To be honest, it's something I continue to work on, as I let go of the need to control everything, plus the need to hold onto money so tight. On the other end of the spectrum, I don't throw money around like there's an endless supply of it. However, I am aware of the mindset I hold around money, its use and its value.

I absolutely adore my mum and I know she did the best she could at the time, with the tools and mindset she had. I also know what may have served her and helped her get through those years, may not serve or support me now. It's about recognising ways of thinking that you have had up to this point, and discerning what to maintain and what to break and let go of. Your mindset can be formed from a repetitive action or comment from others, but it can also be deducted from a single moment - something a teacher said to you, an ex-partner's side remark, or even a portrayal of an image on the media.

The goal with looking into your mindset and where your beliefs have come from is purely to bring awareness to WHAT you are thinking. It is when you have the awareness of what is going on upstairs that you can then CHOOSE your thoughts, what is going to support you and what you therefore attract.

The Physical Hardwiring That Occurs With Your Mindset

When an action or thought is repeated, your brain is literally creating new neural pathways, which are further strengthened every time that action or thought occurs. Simply put (for all of us non-neuroscientists), new nerve connections are made physically in the brain and are organised into circuits. Based on this physical neural wiring, certain situations, or people, trigger your nerves to fire a certain way, prompting hormones, thoughts and feelings which in turn cause a certain reaction or behaviour. This is how habits of thinking, doing, and feeling are created. Hardwiring of certain connections are essential to our day-to-day survival, such as the response of pulling your hand away from a hot element or checking the water temperature before jumping into a bath. Hardwiring is also hugely beneficial in learning a new skill, such as driving. When we first learn to drive, we need to think of every single step in the process. However, after a period of practice and repetition, a new neural pathway is created and we can drive almost automatically, without thought. The same process occurs with your mindset.

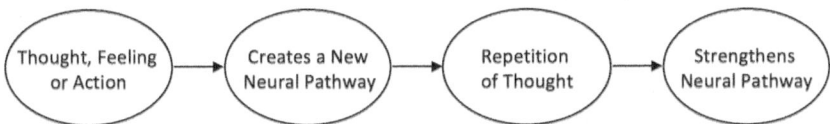

There are many neural circuits that may not serve us now as we are looking for change to create our dream life. The great news is the wiring that no longer serves us can be changed! Scientists now understand the neural plasticity of the brain, meaning it can literally be rewired, breaking and deleting circuits in the brain so it no longer fires in a certain sequence. By rewiring this unwanted neural pathway, replacing it with new thoughts and feelings, we can create new patterns and nerve cell connections in turn changing how we think, act and feel.

Think of our high performance athletes. With belief, visualisation and unwavering thoughts of inspiration, positivity, goal-achievement and success, they are literally creating new neural pathways which will in turn support their physical skills. Through changing their way of thinking - their mindset - they are creating new neural pathways and altering the chemical and hormonal response to support their desired outcomes. They are using their mind to leverage their success.

If this is all too heavy for you, don't panic! The key take-away is you can change your outcomes by firstly changing your frame of thinking. Keep it simple and don't overthink it. What you think about, you bring about. Understand there is scientific evidence proving your mindset is your greatest tool and choose what goes on between your ears. You attract exactly what you're thinking and at any time, you get to choose your thoughts. Creating a new blueprint for success starts with consciously choosing to change the inner landscape of your mind.

The Law of Attraction

You now understand that every thought we have causes our neurons to fire a certain way. In essence, thoughts cause our atoms to vibrate at a certain frequency. It is *this* vibration, or energy, that attracts other like vibrations. This is called the Law of Attraction and is a universal law. A law meaning it is in action whether we consciously are aware of it or not, and also whether we like it or not. Just as the law of gravity, it is constantly in action, it never takes a break and is also non-discriminatory. Like attracts like. So, whether you are thinking negative thoughts and have negative vibration and energy, or if you are thinking positive thoughts and have positive vibration and energy, you will continue to attract, by the law of attraction, more of what you are vibrating.

This universal law works alongside your mindset. You are attracting consciously and unconsciously through your thoughts, which is why it is so important to become aware of, and control your mindset. Your mindset will determine your results through the actions that you take. You simply cannot have a positive attitude and take negative action or have a negative attitude and take positive action. Nor can you say one thing but believe another. This is counter-productive to the desired outcome.

The Secret Sauce

How do you know if your mindset is that of a winner and a successful person or that of someone who thinks the world is against them? The indicator of your mindset is your *Emotional State*.

How you are *feeling* about any given topic is your indicator to which side of the pendulum your mindset is. Feelings of joy, bliss, happiness, excitement, hope when thinking about something indicates you have a positive mindset around that particular topic. Feelings of anger, resentment, fear, hopelessness, jealousy indicate you are on the negative side of the fence. Sure, might sound simple but is it really?

I had an acquaintance many years ago who was the wife of my husband's friend. This person on the outside was bubbly, friendly, seemingly welcoming and interested in me. She was always the first to offer to help and wanted to develop a friendship with me. However, when I was around her, I found myself dealing with feelings of anxiety, frustration and towards the end of the relationship, being annoyed and irritated. Over the time I knew her, it became clear just how jealous she was and insecure in herself, in her life and in her marriage. Whilst she claimed she wanted to maintain a friendship, my feelings were an indication to me that when I was around her, my mindset was that of negativity and pessimism. Not qualities that would help me create my best life nor was she a positive influence in my journey, that's for sure.

Is there a situation or person that makes you feel or behave in a way that is not conducive to what you want to achieve or the person you want to be? Think of what is it about that person or event that triggers you? How is your mindset in that situation? How is your usual mindset when you are not around them? For me, this acquaintance triggered me to feel unvalued and like my voice was not heard. My usual mindset is that of positivity and openness and I found myself feeling anxious, resentful and negative. In trying to create my best life, master my mind, and achieve my goals, this person did not add value. In this instance, there was only one thing to do, which was to disassociate myself and end any contact. It may not be so drastic for you, but it is worth exploring your feelings and mindset with those in your life. I didn't want to feel annoyed or irritated and therefore, attracting more situations to be annoyed and irritated about! The Law of Attraction works regardless of what you are thinking and feeling. Think and surround yourself with negativity and attract the like. Think and surround yourself with positivity and attract the like.

You can choose your thoughts, and therefore your emotions, at any time in an instant. You may be wondering, "But I've been this way my whole life, it's the way I am." Whilst you continue to think a certain way, you will continue to create results that are reflective of that thought process. Change your thinking, your hardwiring, and what you feel and you will change what you attract and create. The formula is simple, not easy. It starts with recognising the limiting thought patterns, as well as the external dialogue, and consciously changing it to support your desires. Becoming consciously aware is the first step to changing the unconscious wiring and creating a different result.

Self-Limiting Beliefs

> *"There is one grand lie - that we are limited. The only limits we have are the limits we believe."*
> **~ Wayne Dwyer**

Aiming high and setting big goals has never been something I struggled with. Have I always achieved them? No. Have I always moved forward? Yes. When I started my online business a few years ago, I set the bar extremely high. I could see other people achieving massive financial and personal goals and I had that feeling deep in my stomach that I too could achieve at that level. Doing the work toward any goal has never been an issue. I come from a family of hard-workers with good work ethic, so I just jumped in with both feet and didn't look back. I soon discovered that whilst I could "do the physical work", I had some serious self-limiting beliefs around success, making money and working in the online space. I could see the business model worked with so many others creating success, so why couldn't I do the same?

I reached out to a childhood family friend, Sherie, whom I had kept in contact with via social media. I saw some posts about her business and about her overcoming blocks in her own life. I had no idea what she did but I resonated with wanting to clear whatever it was that was stopping me. As a Consciousness Coach, Sherie took me through some coaching and helped me uncover the blocks holding me back from truly connecting with my soul. Discovering these deep-seeded blocks was the most incredibly freeing experience, as I wasn't even consciously aware of some of the self-limiting beliefs I had.

Once I had recognised some of the beliefs that were limiting my progress, I was able to then consciously choose more empowering beliefs that were going to support me. Now I'm not at all implying that you simply have to repeat to yourself a positive "new belief" and everything is going to change for you. What I am saying is that firstly by recognising the self-limiting belief, you can then consciously rewire the neural pathways and create a more supportive mindset which will then in turn attract more of what you do want. The first step is in recognising what you truly believe. For me, I had a real block in my belief that I was worthy of success and deserved abundance (in all forms). I can't tell you how massive it was for me to uncover this. I was taking all the actions of a successful person, yet my mindset was that of an unworthy person. I needed to take a look at the beliefs that were indeed repelling the very thing I was trying to attract. After some further peeling back, I was able to absolutely clear that block and replace those beliefs with more empowering, supportive ones. I went from "I don't really believe I deserve this" to "I am the creator of my life and I totally deserve every success I set out to achieve". Strengthening this new belief took time, and conscious effort. Repeating, writing the new belief down, journaling, finding supportive evidence and embodying this new belief rewired my mind and broke the previous *stinking thinking* habit.

ACTION

Identify some thoughts that have limited you in your progress to this point. What stinking thinking can you replace with more powerful ways of thinking? What is going to support you, inspire you and uplift you? What evidence can you find to support this new empowering belief?

Recognise any self-limiting beliefs that are holding you back. How are these no longer serving you? What beliefs have you inherited that are not serving you in creating the life you desire?

Finding Evidence to Support Your New Belief

Your beliefs and mindset are, at any moment, subjective truth. Meaning, they are true for you at a moment in time however, not necessarily true for others, in their physical world, or objectively. In other words, they are not absolute, undeniable laws of nature. When you hold a thought pattern in your mind, your brain looks for evidence to support that thought, thereby strengthening that particular mindset. So, in breaking old stinking thinking and creating new supportive beliefs and a powerful mindset that will catapult you to your goal, you need to find evidence to support it.

Finding evidence to support your new mindset is essential to creating that new neural pathway and breaking the old one. Look for proof in your own life when this new belief was reinforced. When I replaced my old belief with "I am the creator of my life and I totally deserve every success I set out to achieve", I discovered the decisions I had made throughout my adult life have indeed led me to every success I set out to achieve. I have positively been able to create my life, and have always come out on top. Is that deserving? Hell yeah. It wasn't until I looked for evidence that I then found it.

Deciding to change the university degree I was doing. Deciding to pursue an entrepreneurial path over a J.O.B. Deciding to follow my heart, and consequently falling in love with my soulmate. Deciding to take a hobby into a full time business. Deciding to start martial arts as an adult and become number one in the world. Deciding to take responsibility for my success and build an online business. All these decisions have created the evidence for my new belief that I am the creator of my life. The absolute mindset of a winner.

Evidence can also be found in the outside world. Look for others who are doing what you want to do, who have created the success you want to create and who have the belief behind their positive mindset. If need be, borrow their belief and use that to strengthen your own. Soon enough, you will have attracted the results in your own life as evidence yourself and you will have rewired your brain to this new mindset. I absolutely have borrowed other's beliefs and successes and continue to do so as I reach for new goals.

WHAT THEY THINK IS NOT MY BUSINESS

What You See is What You Absorb

I haven't watched the news in almost three years. Sounds crazy, right? Especially around a world health crisis. I do stay informed by doing my own research on world events, however, I choose not to bombard my brain with the negativity and the sensationalism that the media portrays. It's about knowing for yourself, rather than being told in a fearful repetitive way (as is usually the case with the mainstream news and media). Choose how to stay updated and limit the time it takes to update yourself. I'm not saying bury your head in the sand and not have a clue about what's going on, but I am saying be mindful of what you are filling your mind with.

Same goes for social media.

I'm the first to love a good dog video (I'm not a cat lady!), but I also limit my scrolling time. Before you know it, an hour has gone by and you have wasted that time flicking through what other people have had for lunch or what gym pose someone did in the bathroom that day. I love social media, and have built my business around it, but I also choose what I allow into my mind and feed.

Before making this conscious decision, I would spend more time than I care to admit scrolling through the feed and even going and checking out people's profiles. I mean, who hasn't "stalked" someone's profile? What I found though was a feeling of disempowerment, as I subconsciously compared myself to others and their "perfect" social media life. Not all posts made me feel this way, but the ones that did make me feel inferior were the ones I unfollowed first. Honestly, I couldn't handle reading another whinging post, or a rant over something so meaningless such as not getting enough chips in their fast food order. Seriously, THAT was not enriching my life, nor was it helping me be my best self.

MASTER YOUR MIND

These days, I follow people and pages that uplift me, make me smile and that inspire me. You have to guard your mind like it's the most important thing in the world because IT IS! You can't allow negativity and pessimism to creep into the nooks and crannies and then think that you are going to be able to maintain a positive mindset. It simply won't happen.

What is the first thing you do in the morning? Do you grab your phone and check who has commented on your post, or who has sent you a DM? Do you turn on the TV and catch the latest news updates? Or is it journaling, exercising, meditating and pre-framing your mind, setting yourself up for the best start to the day? Which do you think would help with your mindset in the morning - social media / news updates or affirmations, movement and visualisation of your goals? I've done both. I can tell you I'm incredibly more productive PLUS I'm so much happier and in a positive frame of mind with the latter.

Being married to a police officer does make this challenging. It is difficult guarding my mindset when he tells me how his day was dealing with some of the people and circumstances of his job. However, in this case, I wouldn't have it any other way. In fact, it is HIS mindset that changes everything. He is naturally a positive person, and sees his career as his way of keeping the community safe and helping those who have been wronged. I love this about him, and also want him to tell me how he is. Doing the job he does is not easy, and ensuring he doesn't bottle it up is super important to me. Sure, there's some stuff I'd prefer not to know but when this happens, I consciously choose MY thoughts, and if needed, I switch my mindset with the tools I'll share here. I absolutely keep check of my emotions and keep my focus on what I want to attract and the goals I'm working towards.

WHAT THEY THINK IS NOT MY BUSINESS

Steps to Mastering Your Mind

1. Bring attention and awareness to what you are thinking.
   a. Pay attention to every single thought entering and leaving your mind and how you respond emotionally. Does this thought and triggered emotion support you or hinder you? Who influences your mindset and way of thinking?
2. Consciously choose your thoughts.
   a. Break old habits and patterns of thinking by choosing ones that are conducive to the outcome you are trying to create.
3. Physically rewire your brain with new neural circuitry through repetition and finding evidence that supports your mindset.
4. Safeguard and strengthen your mindset by being aware of what you allow to enter it.
5. Attract more of what you want.

Here is a simple diagram to help understand the process:

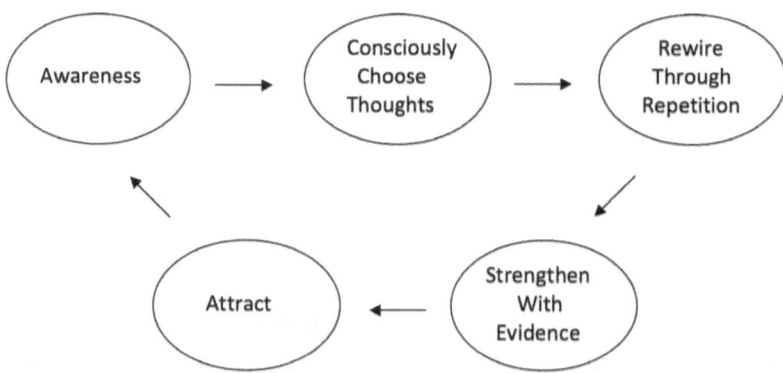

It is absolute truth that you can change your life by changing your mindset. However, that is not all you need to do. It would just be wishful thinking otherwise.

MASTER YOUR MIND

Mastering your mind is key to accomplishing anything. This must be backed with ACTION to make any real change. It is the action you take from the mindset you have that is the real game changer. Take control and master your mind and you are streets ahead in your pursuit of your ideal life and creating lasting change, regardless of what anyone else thinks.

ACTION

Consciously choose your new beliefs. Switch up old beliefs with empowering beliefs that are going to attract more of what you desire. Choose supportive, positive thoughts and find evidence (both from within you and from others) to further strengthen and reinforce these new beliefs.

CHAPTER SUMMARY

- Mastering your mind will almost certainly lead to mastering your life.

- What you think about, what you believe - consciously and subconsciously - draws to it like a magnet the same energetic circumstances. Through self-fulfilling prophecies, you will experience that which you think about.

- The key to determining that your mindset is in alignment with your goals, are your feelings and emotions.

- At any point, you get to choose what you are thinking and what you believe. Break old patterns of thinking and create new neural pathways through repetition.

- Strengthen your mindset with finding evidence both in your own life and those of others of these new beliefs being true.

Mastering your thoughts and becoming a magnet for what you want is absolutely essential in your success journey. But have you really decided in your heart that this is what you want? In Chapter 5, we discover what it means to have a convicted heart, to commit to yourself and your goals, even in the presence of fear.

CHAPTER 5

The Decided Heart

Most people fail at whatever they attempt because of an undecided heart. Should I? Should I not? Go forward? Go back? **Success requires the emotional balance of a committed heart.** *When confronted with a challenge, the committed heart will search for a solution. The undecided heart searches for an escape."*
~ Andy Andrews

This has to be one of the most important keys to success.

When you have truly decided to do something, you cut off all other possibilities and options. You have thrown your hat over the wall and are 100% committed to that path. In 1519, Captain Hermán Cortés

WHAT THEY THINK IS NOT MY BUSINESS

landed in the New World to begin his conquest, and reportedly gave an order for his men to destroy the ships in which they arrived, sending a very clear message that there was no turning back. When you have a decided heart, you have in essence burned your boats, removing any safety net or option to retreat.

Only when you make a definitive decision, can intentional and directed action be taken. Until then, you're simply just moving pieces around a board game. Without a decided heart, you may flip flop between options, not committing to anything, even though you want your situation to change. A lack of decision indicates your unwillingness to back yourself and any action taken from this position is undirected. It is from this unproductive state that thoughts or beliefs such as "I tried that and it didn't work" can arise. How could it work if you first weren't decided in your heart?

Most failures at anything are because of an undecided heart. It is this principle of success that is neglected the most but is one of the most powerful. Do you know someone that just cannot make a decision? Flip flopping between things, never really committing to one path, usually asking friends and family for their opinion on what to do. Maybe this is even you. Most times, those with undecided hearts live in a world of over analysis. Questioning what direction to take, analysing what they should do, trying to predict the outcome of different decisions. Then, when they seem to have decided, they ask others if they made the right decision! Usually this person changes their mind time and time again, going back to the original decision but still not being 100% committed. Over analysis and seeking others' opinions or approval just keeps you stuck in the same position, with no progress or change.

Every journey has its challenges to overcome, and a decided heart will look for solutions. When interest wanes or motivation

THE DECIDED HEART

fades, with a decided heart, you keep going. Without, you look for an escape, any opportunity to do something else. In this case, chances are your heart just isn't in it. You haven't made a clear decision on the path you want to go down. Having a decided heart doesn't mean living without fear. It means the decided heart will courageously move forward, doing what is required to achieve the outcome it believes in, even in the presence of fear.

I regularly speak with motivated individuals looking to create a better life for themselves and for their family. They are keen to change their circumstances, start their own business and build better work-life balance. However, when it comes to deciding and backing themselves, I hear excuses such as, "I really want to but I can't afford it" or "I don't have the money". They have a desire to change but they haven't DECIDED to change. Of course, when investing in anything, money is a consideration. However, in most cases, the decision hasn't been made first. The truth is you don't need the money <u>until</u> you first decide if you want to do something or not. The money is an excuse to not make the initial decision first.

You don't need the money UNTIL you decide to start that business.
You don't need the new house UNTIL you decide to move.
You don't need to find a new job UNTIL you decide to leave your current one.
You don't need that conversation UNTIL you decide you want a better relationship.

Once a decision has been made to do something, money and action come secondary. Things have a way of turning up when you need them. Until you have decided in your heart that you are doing something, you're just merely *thinking* about it.

To Decide or Not to Decide - Is That the Question?

The Latin root of the word decision means "to cut". It originates from the word **decidere** which is a combination of two words: **de** meaning **off** and **caedere** meaning **cut**. To decide literally means *to cut off* - to cut off the majority of options and other courses of action. This is a game changer in your life, as most people cannot make a decision and stick with it. Cutting off other possibilities can feel limiting and perhaps severe, when in fact it's the opposite. Making a decision, without an alternative, is liberating.

> *"Successful people make decisions quickly and change them very slowly (if ever). Unsuccessful people make decisions very slowly, and change them often and quickly."*
> **~ Napoleon Hill**

In today's society, we have so many options that deciding on one thing can almost feel like you're missing out on something else. Your head can spin at the amount of choices available these days. Simply thinking about all the possibilities can be enough to paralyse you. If I choose this, does it mean I miss out on that? In actuality, making a decision frees you from the overabundance of available choices. It is with a decided heart that you then receive everything you want.

The question then becomes whether to decide or not. Will you back yourself, go all in and commit to something, or will you remain wishy-washy, uncertain and affected by others? It's interesting looking at similar words, or synonyms, of decision: conclusion, result, determination, resolution, settlement versus the opposite meaning, or antonyms: disagreement, indecision, refusal, deferment, procrastination, delay. It's fairly obvious then to realise that in not making a decision, you are indeed prolonging the achievement of what you desire. Without decision, and therefore determination and resolution of your vision, you are procrastinating and disagreeing with yourself. Are you after a result, or do you want to defer living your ideal life?

One decision or one doubt can change *everything*.

When you move forward with a decided heart, you immediately start to move in the direction of your goals and things begin shifting in your favour. It is the most powerful action you can take. This is because the focus is taken off the plethora of choices with your energy and focus going to what is needed to get you what you want. The strength of a decided heart will move mountains. The weakness of an undecided heart will dilute your potential and water down your vision.

Taking Control of Your Future Begins in Your Heart

You are reading this book because you want something different in your life. Whether it's to change your career path completely, find love, transform your body physically or to take everything up a notch, you can feel in your heart that you can create the life you want. You want to take control of your life, regardless of what other people think. My question to you is, do you have a decided heart? While the question may seem frivolous, the reality is that the *decision* to pursue exactly what you desire could be the hardest one to make. Many want better lives, better results, healthier lifestyle but rarely is the decision, and hence the burning of the boats, truly made.

WHAT THEY THINK IS NOT MY BUSINESS

When I decided to be an entrepreneur, it was one of the scariest, and equally liberating decisions of my life. I had been tossing between a traditional career (even completing my university degree) and the unknown territory of entrepreneurship for a while, and to be honest, I wasn't 100% sure I could be successful on my own. However, the desire to go for what I wanted - freedom and control of my life and career on my terms - was greater than the fear of missing out on the comfort of so-called job security. Fast forward 20 years and it's obvious there's no such thing as job security. Don't get me wrong, it hasn't been all roses. However, I did burn my boats and made a decision that I would do whatever it took to create the success I believed I could. Through the learning curve (that never ends), I have held onto my end goal, giving myself no way out, and just figuring things out as I go along. It was only with a decided heart that I have stayed the course. The easy path would have been to give up when it got challenging but to be honest, my heart wouldn't allow it.

Most people just aren't up for putting their hearts on the line. They allow opportunities to pass them by, letting the uncertainty of the outcome of their decision paralyse them. They go through life with the fear of what might happen if they take a risk on an opportunity that comes their way. They choose the safety of what they know - their current circumstances - and instead allow their vision and purpose to remain unfulfilled.

A person with a decided heart sees the bigger picture and while the immediate outcome may not be clear, they believe taking this step will lead to the next step. This will in turn lead to the next, and so on toward their goal. Each decision reduces the gap between where they are and what they want. Having a decided heart gives them clarity and opens them to possibilities and circumstances which support their goal. This decided heart guides their actions and they grasp opportunities without hesitation, keeping focused on the bigger picture.

> "At any moment, the decision you make can change the course of your life forever."
> **~ Tony Robbins**

Your Decided Heart Will See You Through

As cliché as it sounds, the journey begins with a single step. That first single step is the decision. If only the equation was as simple as decision + action = success. It's going to get messy, at times it will feel like you are going in the opposite direction and it will challenge you probably in ways you've never been challenged before. The decided heart will see you through to the end. Burning your boats and removing alternatives will make you find a way.

Do you have a decided heart?

Decision and The F word

Throwing your hat over the wall and committing to something is scary AF. I get it. Imagine how those soldiers felt when Captain Hermán Cortés ordered them to destroy their boats? It was literally a "do whatever it takes to survive" situation. For most of us, it won't be a matter of life or death but it also could be, in terms of your dreams surviving or dying. Manage the feelings that come up for you when thinking of cutting off all possibilities, for the outcome will be worth it.

WHAT THEY THINK IS NOT MY BUSINESS

The F word. Fear. Your goal may be so big and scary that just the thought of it makes you sweat. Let me ask you - is the fear around you actually making that vision grounded in reality, or is the fear about going for it and failing?

Fear is the number one emotion that stops us from achieving everything we want in life. It is a hurdle that most cannot get over. Fear can be debilitating, and the only way to overcome it is to expose it again and again. In doing so, it is possible to turn it around so that it will start to work for you. The more you do something, the less fearful it will be and the less hold it will have on you. The first step is the hardest, but can be the most important in kicking fear to the curb.

Fear can be controlled and used to your advantage. For me, I fear not doing something that is going to get me closer to my goals and living my best life, more than the fear of doing it. Ask yourself, what is the worst thing that could happen by doing what I'm fearful of? Without a doubt, it won't be a fatal decision. There is nothing that is impossible to overcome or get through. The more times you face fear, the less power it will have over you.

There's one thing that is 100% certain and that is that fear will always be present. No matter what you do. In making a decision, you will feel fear. In not making a decision, you will still feel fear. However, fear will only have as much power as you give it. We have been conditioned to think when making a decision that there are only two possible outcomes - the right one and the wrong one. Most of us fear choosing a wrong decision. This causes procrastination, when in actual fact by not deciding, we are deciding. You can see how this can turn into a vicious cycle, and how fear can stop us from progressing altogether.

THE DECIDED HEART

"Thinking will not overcome fear but action will."
~ W. Clement Stone

Life is full of choices, which lead to more choices. There are no right or wrong paths to take. If you find yourself on a path that isn't ideal, choose again. It really can be as simple as that. Remove the fear around making the wrong decision because, as long as you learn and grow along the way, you really are winning.

Decide with your heart that you're going to back yourself, you're going all in, there is no turning back, and then do whatever it takes to keep moving forward. Even if you need to readjust your course along the way, the very decision to commit to your goal will sky rocket you forward. If you cannot go "all in" straight away, that's totally ok. Make the decision that you ARE going for it, then take baby steps to get there. Remove any Plan B whilst still moving towards what you want.

"You're not a failure if you don't make it; you're a success because you try."
~ Susan Jeffers

You must be the key player in your own rescue, you must be the dominant force in your actions and the direction you are going. Only you can do what it takes and only you can decide.

ACTION

Are you still sitting on the fence getting splinters in your bum around your decision to pursue your vision? Have you committed to going for it with your heart?

Burn Your Boats. Commit to your goal and yourself by removing all other options. Write a letter or contract to yourself committing to do whatever it takes to fulfil your purpose and why. Only sign it if you are 100% committed.

The power to control your direction begins with you. What is the very next thing you can do today to move forward with your decided heart?

CHAPTER SUMMARY

- When you cut off all other possibilities, any exit strategies, and remove any other options, there's only one thing that can happen...the achievement of exactly what you want.

- You don't need money, time, to leave your job, have that difficult conversation or anything else until you have decided on an outcome FIRST.

- Fear has no power except the power you give it. Expose the fear for what it is, and act in spite of it.

- Have a decided heart and nothing will stop you.

Even with a decided heart, the road to success is bumpy. No-one created anything substantial in their life without having guts and grit. You don't know how strong you are until you are tested. It's all part of the journey! In Chapter 6, we really dive into what it takes to stay the course and see your journey through, no matter what comes your way.

CHAPTER 6

Guts, Grit & Staying The Course

"It's your reaction to adversity, not adversity itself that determines how your life's story will develop."
~ Dieter F. Uchtdorf

There's no getting out of this life unscathed. Shit happens and it happens to everyone. There's no other way to put it.

If you think you will be able to avoid acquiring some bumps and bruises along the way, you're sorely mistaken. The journey to anything is never a straight one although, wouldn't it be nice if it was? Obstacles, challenges and difficulties will be put in our way on the path to our goal. Some come disguised as another opportunity, a person with "your best interest at heart", or others can be downright game-stoppers such as illness or death of a

WHAT THEY THINK IS NOT MY BUSINESS

loved one. Many things will happen in our lifetime that will test us, trial us and put extreme pressure on us. You will get thrown curveballs and you WILL ask yourself, "Is this all really worth it?"

Having problems is not the problem. It is the way you look at problems that will slow you down, if not halt you completely. Problems are an opportunity to learn, grow and develop your tenacity. They are put there to test your will and resiliency, your commitment and grit to seeing it through to the end. They are essentially the stepping stones towards success. It's when your back is up against the wall, when the pressure is turned right up, that transformation occurs.

It is because of problems and tribulations that we become stronger and develop resiliency and confidence we never knew we had. It is not our job to avoid challenges, or other people. It is our job to overcome these hardships to learn and grow. While the end goal can give us a target to aim for, the real winning outcome is the person you become along the way. With an increased tenacity, resilience and determination, you will build an immunity to that level of stress or problem, giving you even more strength on your journey. Overcoming challenges will give you those lessons needed to move forward and grow.

In the beginning of my online business, I was so heavily focused on the results I wanted to create that when I hit my first road block - other people's opinions on my business - it shook me. How could they not see what I see? How could they think it was anything but an unbelievable opportunity to create an amazing life? I was floored by some of the opinions that came flying at me, until I remembered *what they think is not my business*. Don't get me wrong, this didn't happen in an instant. It took me revisiting my goals, borrowing the belief of others creating results in the business, and reviewing my own beliefs about myself and success before I was able to confidently say, I don't care what other people think. In hindsight, I am glad they had those opinions if only for my chance to prove them wrong! This experience has made me stronger and far more resilient when faced with similar situations, and I can actually appreciate that lesson. I realised over my life up to that point, I had allowed other's opinions to shift my course of action, so overcoming this problem has been a huge lesson and blessing.

> *"Grapes must be crushed to make wine. Diamonds form under pressure. Olives are pressed to release oil. Seeds grow in darkness. Whenever you feel crushed, under pressure, pressed, or in darkness, you're in a powerful place of transformation and transmutation. Trust the process."*
> **~ Lalah Delia**

Feeling pressure and facing difficulties along the journey is expected. Shying away from problems, or allowing challenges to completely derail you, will only keep you where you are. Your life will remain unchanged. Other people, or situations, will continue to have control over you. You will continue to move from one shiny object to another until something happens and you move on again. You will remain at the effect of others and outside influences. Your goals will continue to move and change and ultimately you won't create the life you truly desire.

I'm sorry if you are going through a tough time at the moment. It sucks. However, just know it will pass, if you remain resolved and persistent. You will come out the other side stronger, more attuned to the actions you need to take, with greater tenacity, resilience and grit to continue your journey. You will have a more enriched life because of these problems and looking back, you will be able to see the grace in them.

ACTION

List out challenges or obstacles you have faced along your journey so far.

Were you able to overcome them? If they are still blocking your progress, try looking at it from another angle such as to what can you learn? Are there skills you need to further develop? What resources or people can you draw on to help you through?

Resiliency, Tenacity, Guts and Grit

While I was studying at university, I worked at the local gym. I was only 19 and while I had played some sport growing up, I definitely was not in peak physical state. I started training at the gym and soon felt muscles I didn't even know existed! Over time, the strength in my muscles grew. The more I trained, the fitter and stronger I became. Soon, I had completely transformed my body. What was once a difficult exercise, no longer challenged me at the same intensity. In order to continue to improve, I needed to increase the intensity to further challenge my body. The level of strength in my muscles was in direct proportion to how much I used them.

The exact same principle applies to building and developing your 'muscles' of resilience and tenacity. They need to be worked and tested in order to be strengthened. The more you use them, the stronger they get! Think of a baby learning to walk. Imagine if the baby was able to pull itself up using a chair into a standing position, took one step away, fell, hurt themselves and resolved they will never be able to walk. It just doesn't happen. The baby, falling time and time again, hurting itself in the process, gets up every single time and keeps trying until they can walk. And then they don't stop walking! The tenacity of the baby to walk is incredible despite the challenges it faces along the way.

"Never give up" is an overused cliché but guess what, it's true! The only time failure can exist is when you stop trying completely. Most times, the challenges we face along the way are simply testing our commitment and resolve to the goal. How badly do you really want it?

JK Rowling was rejected 12 times for her Harry Potter manuscript before being picked up by a publisher. According to Forbes, JK Rowling is the second highest paid author in the world and in 2020 made a whopping $60M. Imagine if she had given up after the first or even the tenth rejection! The world would have missed out on the wonderful wizard tale and JK Rowling would still be on government benefits.

Find it in yourself to get to the end. Determination and grit are bigger weapons than anything else. Building mental resilience means there's nothing that could stop you. Every day is a challenge. It's whether you have the mental fortitude to stay the course that is the difference maker.

It takes guts and grit to see something through to the end. A good friend of mine, Sandy, used to tell me all the time, "Anyone can start strong. It's how you finish it that counts." As a WMC Welterweight

WHAT THEY THINK IS NOT MY BUSINESS

Australian Muay Thai Boxing Champion, Sandy is a true example of having the guts and grit to see something to the end. Sandy was 32 years of age and already a mum when she started Muay Thai Boxing. It was only with the unrelenting tenacity and resilience that she was able to defeat opponents almost half her age and win championships over the ten years she competed. When Sandy started her incredibly gruelling training regime, she started out blazing. She told me, "Anyone can start strong." Through building her mental strength, having relentless tenacity and undeniable resilience, Sandy finished her career just as strong as she started. Many other athletes who didn't have that level of grit would have given up far earlier.

How strong is your resilience and tenacity? Have you been known in the past to start something, and give up just as quickly? Do you have all good intentions to complete something only to be taken out of the game at the first, or even at the tenth, problem you face? Do you shy away from challenges along the way, or do you face them head on? Do you finish what you start, or even do what you say you're going to do? The strength of your tenacity and resilience is in direct alignment to the strength of your fire burning. Is your why strong enough to push through hurdles along the way?

What Can Take You Out of The Game

What really is strong enough to take you out of the game completely? Think about that for a moment. Is there anything that is unachievable if you <u>really</u> wanted it bad enough and just kept going?

The stronger your fire, the deeper your why, the less opportunity for an obstacle to get in your way. In my journey of entrepreneurship, it was my deep fire and why that kept me going when I really wanted to quit. Being told 'no' over and over can dampen your spirits but taking the moment to connect with the bigger picture and what I truly believe I could create, kept me going. Unfortunately, some people just can't find a way to push through a challenging time and give up just as they're close to breaking to the other side.

> *"Giving up on your goal because of one setback is like slashing your other three tyres because you got a flat."*
> **~ Unknown**

Shiny Object Syndrome (SOS) is a behaviour described as chasing anything that's shiny or new, jumping from one thing to another without seeing anything through to the end. This is particularly common in my industry. Some people start their own business because they see the bigger picture, they want to take control of their career, they want to create better results in their life. They start out full of enthusiasm, spruiking their love of their new business, and setting big goals. Then they hit a rough patch - multiple objections, no leads coming in or they have had an advertisement disapproved. They question themselves and the business. They then find another business that looks exciting, and soon enough they've jumped across into another opportunity. More times than not, they will face the same problems, same challenges and same hardships that come with building ANY business - traditional or non-traditional. They will continue moving from opportunity to opportunity, thinking it is the business that isn't working. Rather, it is simply the lack of tenacity, resilience, guts or grit that is the real problem.

WHAT THEY THINK IS NOT MY BUSINESS

Whatever you want to do, whether it's to start your own business, write a book, find love, change your career, have a family, build a real estate portfolio or become a self-made millionaire, you're going to get bumps and bruises along the way. You will be faced with challenges that seem insurmountable. You may have friends or family who don't support you. It's not what hurdles you face along the way, it's what you do in spite of those hurdles that will make the difference. Will you keep going and find a way regardless?

You have the power and ability to change anything in your life, to create anything and to live any way you choose. Only with tenacity and resilience will you keep going when the going gets tough. Get enough skin in the game, play full out and don't let anything stop you. You can do it.

Remember, be kind to yourself. At the start of my entrepreneurial journey, I would put so much pressure on myself to get stuff done, to make things happen, that when I hit a road block along the way, I would put more pressure on myself to overcome it. Sometimes, you just need to walk away from what you're trying to do. Take a breath and give yourself some self-love. Chances are it's not going to get worse by taking some time out. You can come back to it with a clear mind and perhaps a different perspective. You're doing a great job, and heck if you're facing challenges...WELL DONE! It means you're actually in the game and not sitting on the sidelines waiting for life to change. You're creating your life your way. There are no obstacles big enough that can stand in your way, if you have the guts and grit to see it through.

GUTS, GRIT & STAYING THE COURSE

"I want to be in the arena. I want to be brave with my life. And when we make the choice to dare greatly, we sign up to get our asses kicked. We can choose courage or we can choose comfort, but we can't have both. Not at the same time."
~ Brené Brown

ACTION

Make a commitment to seeing your goals through to the end. Start strong AND finish stronger, regardless of what comes along your way. Vow to staying the course and welcome challenges along the way, knowing they are part of the journey and that nothing has the power to take you out of the game completely.

CHAPTER SUMMARY

- Anyone can start strong. It's how you finish that counts.

- Resilience, determination and tenacity are bigger weapons than any talent or skill.

- You have the power to get through anything. The only time failure occurs is when you give up altogether.

- You will get dirty, you will fall down and you can get up with strong resolve, resilience and tenacity.

Staying the course and walking the walk requires strong resilience and a tenacious attitude. Of course, these are only a few pieces of the pie that make up the total equation. Everything takes effort and consistency. From building a business or career, to having a long-term loving relationship, to being in peak physical shape, it takes being consistent. In Chapter 7, we break down this secret to sure fire success - the significance of Consistency.

GUTS, GRIT & STAYING THE COURSE

Despite the difficulties of raising two daughters on her own, my older sister and I always knew how much we were loved. I am a strong woman because a strong woman raised me.

If I could tell my 10-year-old self anything, it would be that you can truly be, do and have anything you want. Stop caring about what other people think and never give up or stop dreaming big.

WHAT THEY THINK IS NOT MY BUSINESS

After completing my University degree, I soon realised that my true desire was to be an entrepreneur and live a life of my crafting, assisting others do the same.

Opening our first full-time martial arts centre, Total Self Defence Academy, was a dream come true. Over 13 years, we grew our business to four locations with more than 400 students. Today, we continue to teach families in our local school halls, after the global pandemic forced the closure of our full-time club.

December 23rd 2019 - The day I became the Highest Ranked female in the world in Hapkido Moohakkwan.

A truly momentous day showing my girls that with consistency and perseverance anything is possible. Grading alongside my girls in 2019 - I achieved 5th Degree Black Belt, while Brooklyn attained her 3rd Degree Black Belt and Indiana became a Bo Dan Black Belt. A day I will never forget.

WHAT THEY THINK IS NOT MY BUSINESS

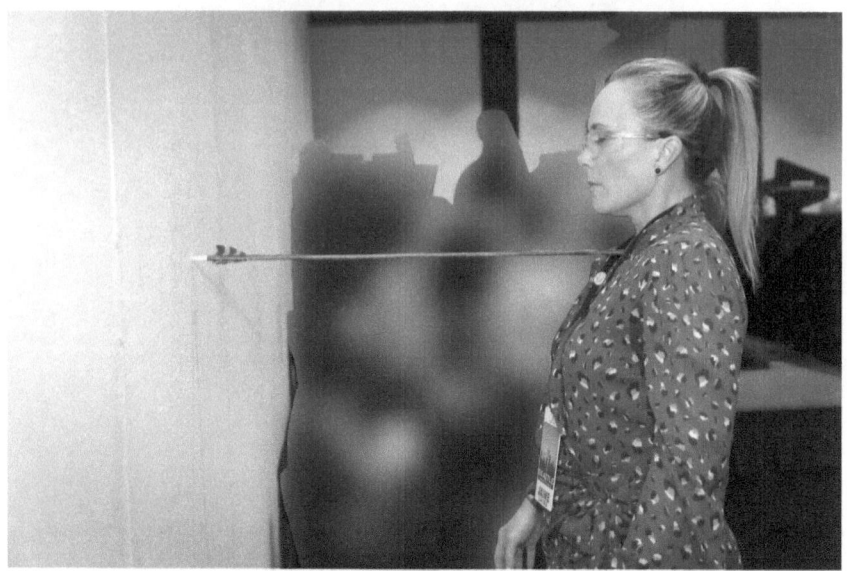

What this photo doesn't show are the tears streaming down my face from absolute fear and disbelief over what I am about to do. Breaking an arrow with the soft part of my throat has to be one of the scariest things I've ever done. This photo is representative of what it takes to overcome anything - confidence, determination and a resolute willpower that you can, and will, do it.

Being recognised as a "Rising Star" within the company I partner with in my online business. I am so grateful to have been acknowledged for the leadership and work I bring to my organisation and the company.

My greatest achievements by far are my girls and my family. They are my why and the driving force behind everything I do.

CHAPTER 7

The Secret to Sure-Fire Success

What makes someone create success? Is it Ambition? Luck? Persistence? Determination? Intelligence? These definitely are key ingredients to a successful outcome of any goal but the one key element of success that is more important than any other is *Consistency*.

I have been honoured to coach men and women for over 20 years in various areas from health and fitness, sales and marketing, life coaching to business coaching. In the beginning, excitement is next level. Enthusiasm is at an all-time high and they're ready to make change. They jump into their coaching, and very soon start taking big bold action towards what they want. They may get up earlier, stay up later, sacrifice a few things to work on their goal and their motivation is palpable. Then slowly, things start to decline. They may sleep in longer, they miss a session or two, skip on a few action steps they said they would do, allow themselves to slip back into old habits and before you know it, they may even stop trying altogether. Time and time again, I have witnessed this cycle. The excitement and enthusiasm they once had turns into frustration and impatience and they give up. Sound familiar?

On the other hand, those who have successfully achieved what they set out to do, did so with one thing in common. They applied the secret to sure-fire success.

Consistency

It's not really about luck or talent, it is about being consistent in what you do. Consistency is the secret to creating success in any area of your life. Any athlete will attest to the hours upon hours of training they went through to achieve a high level of performance. Any musical artist will affirm the countless hours they practised refining their skill. Any successful business owner will verify the results they created were from action steps they repetitively took over time. Anyone who has improved their health and fitness, lost weight or gained strength did so because of their regular, unfailing action. No one who has achieved any level of success did so by attempting something once, or twice. In his book Outliers, Malcolm Gladwell states it takes approximately 10,000 hours to master a skill. While there are a number of reports disputing this theory, it emphasises the fact that to achieve anything, it takes consistency and discipline over time.

> "Success doesn't come from what you do occasionally. It comes from what you do consistently."
> **~ Marie Forleo**

THE SECRET TO SURE-FIRE SUCCESS

Those who do slow down or stop taking action toward their goal, do so because of a number of reasons. They don't see immediate results. They allow others' opinions to dampen their enthusiasm. They let outside forces take control. They yo-yo or continue a pattern of stop-start. Quite often, this leads to frustration and the end of their pursuit for a better life.

A powerful representation of the effect of consistency that I have heard comes from one of the owners of the company I partner with, Rachel. She tells the story of a plane taking off. Imagine sitting on the tarmac at the end of a runway about to take off. The pilot starts the engine, powers up the plane, and hits the throttle. The plane shoots off down the runway and the pilot decides to draw back the throttle and the plane stops. It is already half way down the run way when it stops suddenly. The pilot decides to take off again, however cannot do so from this halfway point as there's not enough runway to get the speed up to take off. He needs to go back to the end of the runway to start all over again.

This is such a strong demonstration of the power of consistency. For when you stop doing something, your momentum and results stop. In most cases, to start again, you will need to go all the way back to the beginning.

I too, am guilty of lacking consistency from time to time. This is not something I typically let myself get away with but I most recently experienced this with respect to my health and fitness. I have always been active from a young age. I played team sports through my childhood and became a group fitness instructor and personal trainer in my early 20s. Throughout my two pregnancies, I taught classes up to almost giving birth, and I returned to teaching about six to eight weeks later. I've had two knee arthroscopes where I needed to rehabilitate for about 12 weeks each time,

WHAT THEY THINK IS NOT MY BUSINESS

but apart from that, I haven't ever stopped or injured myself to the point where I couldn't be active. After I stopped teaching and coaching, I took up CrossFit and with my training partner, Al, socially competed in a few comps. I was strong, fit and feeling great. Then I stopped.

I suffered an injury, and along with lockdowns due to the global pandemic, I was out of the game for a good six months or so. I had developed a very strong consistent routine in my life around my health and fitness however, by not being able to go to the gym (or do what I wanted to with my injury), my consistency stopped. When lockdowns were lifted and my injury healed, my motivation was at a 20 year low and I had lost all confidence in myself and exercising in the gym. Sounds crazy right, especially after 20 odd years of living in a gym environment.

I reached a point where I yearned for that feeling of confidence in myself, feeling fit and healthy and I knew I wanted to start being active again. I started walking, then running, and then joined a Boot Camp program to try to reintroduce myself back into exercise. What a shock to the system that was! I literally felt like I was exercising for the very first time. My muscle strength was near non-existent, my fitness was in the toilet and it hurt...a lot!

Over time, I began to get stronger. I began to look forward to the next day to exercise. And gradually my health and fitness returned. But it didn't return with just training once after my six month hiatus. Nor did it return after two, three or ten sessions. I didn't go into the first session with an incredibly high level of intensity and expect to feel like I did before I stopped. Let me tell you, it would have been easy to not even go back after the first class. However, slowly it improved to the point where I was feeling great, both physically and mentally, again.

THE SECRET TO SURE-FIRE SUCCESS

This was a huge lesson to learn. I had spoken to clients, team members as well as family and friends about consistency over the years, but had never experienced it like this before. I had a new appreciation for this secret to sure fire success more so than I had before.

"Long term consistency trumps short term intensity."
~ Bruce Lee

Being consistent in your actions, thoughts and behaviours is such a simple concept, yet why do so many people struggle with it? Take New Year resolutions for example. As January 1 rolls around, people are eager to make the year ahead different from the last. They set health goals, financial goals, business goals, personal goals, travel goals, spiritual goals, family goals, the list goes on. They take action and firmly believe this is the year it's all going to happen! By February 1, a staggering 80% of these new year goals have faded. 80%!

A big part of my sporting background is in martial arts. I started training in my late 20s and quite quickly developed a love and passion for it. When I started, I wanted to compete and had a vision of winning gold medals and being number one. Yes, when I set goals, I don't do things by the half. My goals are always big.

Over the years, whilst I remained fairly consistent in my training, my priorities shifted. My hubby and I started a family and decided to pursue our vision of having a full time academy. As life got busy being a mum and building a business, my goal of becoming number one in our martial art was pushed further away. Over time, I did however, remain consistent in my training and wanted to be a demonstration to my girls (and students) of the power, strength and possibility of women in martial arts.

It was these consistent actions that I took - week in, week out - that enabled me to create the results I have. Almost 17 and a half years after I started training, I became the *highest ranked female in the world* in our discipline, Hapkido Moohakkwan. What was even more astonishing to me, was that when I graded for my 5th degree Black Belt, I had no idea that by doing so, it would make me number one globally. I was overwhelmed and so surprised when I found out my ranking, however I did set that intention 17 years ago and took consistent action, right?

Why The Struggle?

If consistency is key to achieving anything, why do so many people struggle with it? I believe it is a skill that is learned and developed. In a world of instant gratification, society on a whole has become accustomed to getting what they desire immediately. From ordering food to be delivered straight to your door, to making purchases with companies that allow you pay it off, to even having surgery to attain an ideal weight. Things are so readily available that to take consistent action on something that doesn't deliver instant results is often difficult.

Impatience is simply the reason why most goals are never achieved. Living in the short term causes most to miss amazing opportunities to create lasting change in the long term. In other words, they don't see the point in continuing those actions long term when they can't see results in the short term. Imagine if Michael Jordan got impatient with developing his skills on the basketball court? While I'm sure there were moments or even periods of frustration in building his sporting career, Michael consistently practised and practised in spite of any obstacle or length of time. Having a dream bigger than the immediate frustrations he was feeling kept him consistent in his training, and therefore got him the results he wanted.

> "I've always believed that if you put in the work, the results will come. I don't do things half-heartedly. Because I know if I do, then I can expect half-hearted results."
> **~ Michael Jordan**

Remember the shiny object syndrome? Those who suffer from this syndrome get distracted easily and lack focus or discipline in seeing something through to the end. Living in the 21st century exposes us to many distractions every second. Even just sitting down to write this chapter, I found myself aimlessly checking social media and emails. How often have you caught yourself being distracted from what you wanted to do? Being consistent is all about maintaining focus on your desired goal, and being disciplined enough to not allow distractions to take you off course.

Show Up No Matter What

The key to success in anything is taking consistent action. Consistency is all about repetition. Repetition leads to habits being formed. The habit of taking action builds incremental progress and improvement, over time, towards what you want. It's not about short term results. It takes commitment to remain consistent, even when things don't seem to be improving. It is in doing the little things consistently, that add up to the big improvements.

WHAT THEY THINK IS NOT MY BUSINESS

Consistency and repetition also lead to developing the necessary skills required for your goal. For me, the online business world was a whole new arena and I needed to develop new skills of online marketing and digital advertising in order to get my business off the ground. In the beginning, there were days where I wanted to throw my computer out the window. It was like learning a new language. However, I remained consistent. Every day, I worked on improving myself. I placed a new ad. I tried a different ad copy. I trialled different images. By repeating this consistently, I was able to develop the skills needed to be an effective online marketer and now be able to teach others to do the same.

There really is no such thing as overnight success. It is because of the actions taken consistently, that habits are formed and skills are developed to create success. Show up every day, even on days you don't feel like doing it, or when you don't feel like you're making any progress. Being consistent in your actions comes down to discipline.

By showing up and doing what needs to be done consistently, you are affirming how bad you want your goal. Make giving up not an option. Commit to the journey - however long or short that may be - if you really want something bad enough.

There is only one person responsible for whether you achieve something or not. You. Sure, you may have coaches and a support network to help you along the way, but ultimately your success is only determined by you and the action you take consistently.

THE SECRET TO SURE-FIRE SUCCESS

Developing Consistency

Just like building your resilience and tenacity "muscles", consistency must be developed and strengthened. If you are someone who struggles to be consistent, start small! Pick something such as setting the alarm 15 minutes earlier every day. Or even going to bed 15 minutes earlier. Just pick something that you CAN maintain for at least 21 days - the time it takes to create a habit. Building the belief in yourself that you can do something consistently is the confidence you require to hit the larger goals.

Developing consistency where it becomes a habit, takes time. Once you have decided on pursuing something and have committed to the journey, start. Make a list of the action needed to accomplish what you want and be accountable to yourself (or someone else if it helps). If your goal is to lose 5 kgs, what needs to happen for you to achieve that? Start an exercise program. Plan out your meals. Reduce snacking and take out. Break it down further by integrating into your life. How often will you exercise? When will you exercise? Will you ask someone to be your exercise buddy? Will you pre-cook some meals or pack your lunch the night before? What snacks or take out will you reduce? Will you hire a trainer, join a gym or do your own thing? The goal here is to break down what needs to happen <u>consistently</u>. It's no good deciding to lose 5 kgs and not have a plan of what actions are needed to take. How can you be consistent if you don't have a plan?

It's really important to ensure you count your wins along the way. This will help maintain your focus and motivation when you don't see immediate results. Keeping your vision on your end goal is critical, but also be present to what you have achieved in the process. Create a plan, work the plan consistently, and maintain a steady focus.

WHAT THEY THINK IS NOT MY BUSINESS

What if you don't know what actions are needed to achieve your goal? Research what other successful people do consistently. What habits have they formed? What are the non-negotiables for them on a daily, weekly, monthly basis? Success leaves clues, so find out what others are doing to achieve results and get moving on building your consistent action.

"It's not what we do once in a while that shapes our lives. It's what we do consistently."
~ Tony Robbins

ACTION

How can you be more consistent in your actions? What are others doing consistently to get the results you desire? Don't try to change too much at once. Build small changes into your routine that you can do consistently and create the habit of continuing. There's no point doing something once or twice. Consistency is key to long term success.

Clear Road Blocks Before You Reach Them

Living in a world of distractions, instant gratification and impatience, it would be a good idea to recognise what habits to avoid, especially if you are someone who is easily taken off course. For me, I recognised I was easily distracted with playing games on my phone which also ate away at valuable time I could have used to do something productive. So, they were deleted. This not only

THE SECRET TO SURE-FIRE SUCCESS

freed up time, but also created space in my mind to focus on the actions that would create the results I wanted.

How are you easily distracted? Do you seek instant gratification or are you impatient when it comes to wanting something? Consistency works for both positive action and also negative action. Imagine having apple pie and ice cream every night for dessert. Whilst you may not see the effect of this immediately, or even after a week or two, over the long term, weight will be gained, blood sugar will most probably increase and due to creating a habit of having high sugar dessert, chances are you will be craving more and more. Make sure you're taking positive action that is going to take you closer to your goals, rather than further away.

I have a vision board in my office with pictures of all my short and long term goals. In moments when I'm feeling impatient, or even tired of not seeing immediate results, I am quickly reminded of what I want to create and I can pull myself up on my little pity party and just get on with it. I ask myself, "What is one thing I can do right now to get me closer to what I want?" Having the long term goal in focus, I am then able to bring my attention back to what needs to be done in the moment. Maintain your focus on individual action steps needed for the long term vision in your mind. Focusing too much on the big goal can be overwhelming and cause inaction because it can seem so far away. Bring the attention to the smaller steps taken on a regular basis to alleviate any sense of disconnect to the big picture.

Possible road blocks include your perceptions and feelings about other people. This has definitely been a game stopper for me in the past. In these instances, look at the results these particular people are getting in their life. Are they living the life you are trying to create? I'd bet my last dollar they're not. So, why worry about

WHAT THEY THINK IS NOT MY BUSINESS

what they think? You do you and do what it takes to change your life, despite what others think.

Being consistent in the actions needed to achieve any goal truly is the sure-fire secret to success. It is the key to creating lasting change and getting the results you desire. The formula is simple to do, but also simple not to do. Commit, make a plan, work the plan...consistently. Will you be consistent?

CHAPTER SUMMARY

- If you are serious about creating lasting change in your life, the secret sure-fire way to success is in being consistent.

- Just like a plane trying to take off, you cannot stop-start and expect to get off the ground.

- Things take time. Keep your eye on the ball and show up every day, even on days you don't feel like it.

- Prepare for, and clear any road blocks before you reach them.

- Build consistency into your routine gradually. Trying to change your whole life in one day or week will not last. Focus on creating lasting habits that over time will bring you the results you are after.

Being consistent will create results every time. It trumps short term intensity and produces lasting change. These are all necessary for your success in anything. In Chapter 8, you will discover how we are gently being guided by a higher power on the path we take. Things never randomly happen, everything happens for a reason.

CHAPTER 8

Sizzling Synchronicities

Stop! Slow Down! Wrong Way! Keep Left! Give Way! We see signs everywhere when we're driving telling us what to do, what not to do and where to go. If only we received signs like this in our life journey. Or do we?

> *"In every moment, The Universe is whispering to you. You are constantly surrounded by signs, coincidences, and synchronicities all aimed at propelling you in the direction of your destiny."*
> **~ Denise Linn**

We are all being guided by something greater than us. Nothing happens by accident and whether you recognise its existence or not, this guiding presence is around us all of the time. There are too many meaningful coincidences or synchronistic moments that are unexplainable. Countless occurrences that are inscrutable and cannot be summed up as phenomena. That can be difficult to accept when shitty things happen in our lives, but for one reason or another, bigger than we realise, there is something governing our experience in this lifetime. Call that what you will - God, Universe, Spirit, Angels, Soul, Higher Self or Power - the name in this context doesn't matter. This isn't about being religious but it is about being aware of what is showing up for you. When you start to pay attention to what is coming to you as signs and sizzling synchronicities, it's so damn exciting and can propel your life forward in ways you never imagined. Synchronicities act as a breadcrumb trail to what we truly desire and are magical and inspiring happenings in our lives. For simplicity, from this point forward, we will refer to this guidance as The Universe.

I have my feet firmly planted on the ground but I absolutely believe there is a higher force that none of us truly understand, guiding us. It's up to our conscious minds to recognise the signs and hints along the way. These signs can also be known as déjà vu, random occurrences, a feeling, a hunch, a thought you have or even a dream. They can come to you in various forms through song, animals, someone you meet randomly, quotes you hear over and over, patterns or numbers repeated (e.g. 111 or 12:12), symbols or unexpected phone calls, to name a few. These signs can be easily observed just as much as they can be ignored and have the power to shape your path and destiny.

> "Synchronicity is an ever present reality for those who have eyes to see."
> **~ Carl Jung**

SIZZLING SYNCHRONICITIES

Have you been somewhere or have been doing something for the first time but had the feeling you've been there before, or have done whatever it is you're doing before? Almost like *in another life* you've done this? Maybe it's meeting someone that feels so familiar to you that it's quite eerie. I have had this happen to me countless times throughout my life and while some call it déjà vu, I absolutely feel like it's a powerful wink from The Universe letting me know I'm on the right path. It is a confidence booster and raises my energy and vibration reaffirming I'm on the path I'm meant to be on, doing what I'm meant to be doing, and it's all working out.

Overlooking the signs on your journey can lead to missing the magic along the way, missing the beauty in this greater guidance. As we all know, things can get tough and such synchronicities can help see you through to the other side. They can be nudges to change course, or open you up to new possibilities. When you just don't know what direction to take, they can guide you along the way and make you see things you weren't aware of.

What is A Sizzling Synchronicity?

Carl Jung, a psychoanalyst, first coined the term "synchronicity" in a 1930 lecture, which he explained as two events that appear related occurring simultaneously with no direct cause and effect relationship (Jung, 1952). That is, things that are unexplainably coincidental and have meaning to the person as opposed to a coincidence that has no meaning. Such as, it's your loved one's anniversary, you turn on the radio and their favourite song plays, or thinking of a person you haven't spoken to in a while and they call you randomly.

WHAT THEY THINK IS NOT MY BUSINESS

It's important to have a clear understanding of synchronicities, as they are powerful reminders of the guidance you are receiving. Plus, it's a hell of a lot of fun noticing them! While there is no scientific proof whether synchronicities are valid or not, it is 100% subjective truth for the individual, their experience and opinion. Remember, it needs to be meaningful to *you* to be synchronistic to you. The journey is individual, unique and different for each of us, and while we might engage others along the way, it remains purposeful just to you.

My journey to becoming a published author was a synchronistic event. I had been thinking of writing a book for about 15 years but hadn't taken any action steps to achieving that goal. Scrolling on Facebook one day, I came across an advertisement for a seminar on how to become an author. Sign? I hadn't googled anything to do with writing a book prior so I couldn't blame the algorithm (or Big Brother?!) for displaying the advertisement in my newsfeed. I thought, "This could be interesting" so I entered my details. I had no idea where to begin, how to write a book or how to publish it so I went in open and ready to learn, as I'd had the goal of becoming an author on my vision board for one and a half decades!

This two hour seminar was eye opening. First of all, it cemented in my mind my goal of becoming an author and also highlighted the fact that I had no idea about the publishing world. I decided to go with my gut instinct and sign up with the Ultimate 48 hour Author who were a one stop shop for editing, publishing and marketing your book.

When I decided to finally write this book, it was scary! Like anything new, I was filled with feelings of uncertainty, hesitation and doubt. However, when I saw the advertisement, I didn't think twice, instead

SIZZLING SYNCHRONICITIES

thought it would be interesting to investigate this sign; what did I have to lose?

After committing to writing my book, filled with uneasiness and an unknowing, I was at the hairdressers and just so happened to mention I was writing a book. It's important to note here that I usually do not speak of what I'm doing to anyone until I've done it or am in the thick of it. It's just not my style to talk myself up when I haven't actually done (or am doing) something. At this stage, I hadn't even written my first word. I had an idea of what I wanted to write about, but had yet to put pen to paper. So, to say, "I'm writing a book" was massively outside of my comfort zone.

As my hairdresser asked me questions, I got more comfortable with talking about it and probably a little more excited, as in my mind, I was affirming, "Yes! I am an author and it's going to happen". The lady beside me interrupted and told me she too in fact had written three books, and proceeded to confirm that I had done the right thing by going with the publishing company, as she had tried self-publishing her first book and wasted a tonne of money doing so. Sign? She then shared some great tips on marketing my book, where I should go and what I should do to get it out there. When I left the hairdresser, I couldn't take the smile off my face. It was sure fire sign I was on the right path, I had made the right decision and now had the confidence to push forward! Now to anyone else, this synchronistic moment would have meant nothing. For me, filled with doubt if I had done the right thing, could I do it, should I have self-published etc, having this conversation, meeting this lady and hearing the message she gave me, was a powerful wink from The Universe, "You've got this girl."

Where have you had synchronistic moments that perhaps you dismissed as a mere coincidence with no deeper meaning?

Perhaps it was a conversation, or seeing a particular animal or car repeatedly? A certain song or a number of songs with similar messages? Receiving an email or seeing an advertisement on your social media? Start paying attention to what is happening around you and how beautifully you are being guided and gently nudged.

> *"Don't dismiss the synchronicity of what is happening right now finding its way to your life at just this moment. There are no coincidences in The Universe, only convergences of Will, Intent, and Experience."*
> **~ Neale Donald Walsch**

Signs?! What Signs?

Don't think you receive signs? Whether you're sceptical or not, I encourage you to be open and take action on signs you do receive. The key is the personal connection the sign has to you. Welcome synchronicities into your awareness and take action when they do. See where it leads you and what other avenues come up because of them.

Here are seven simple mindset shifts and basic concepts to welcome more synchronistic moments into your life:

1. Quieten the mind.
Studies show that we can have over 6000 thoughts per day and with so many things demanding our attention, it can be challenging to decipher what to notice or dismiss. Taking the time to deliberately stop the flow of thought and incoming messages is super important to being able to allow the right messages and signs to get in. Take the time daily, or whenever you feel the need,

to sit still, close your eyes, focus on your breath, and try not to think of anything in particular. This is definitely a practice that you will get better at the more times you do it. When you think of something, allow the thought to float away and bring your awareness back onto your breath and relaxing your muscles. If you are going to think of anything during this process, think of your intention (in Step 2).

2. Form a clear intention.
If you feel you aren't receiving signs or having synchronistic moments, you may need to get clear on exactly what it is you want. What are you wanting guidance on? What are you wanting to create and what is your end goal? What challenges are you trying to overcome? Be crystal clear on what it is you are seeking. I knew for 15 years that I wanted to be an author. When I became crystal clear on my end goal, signs appeared for me. Journal and describe in as much detail as possible what you truly want guidance on, and why.

3. Be mindful & aware.
Be present in the moment. Rushing around is normal these days and so bring your attention and awareness to what you are doing, who you are with, what conversations you're having, what is in your surroundings, and any repetitive symbols, songs or messages. Truly open your eyes and heart and connect to the moment, even if that is sitting in traffic. This practice will help raise your level of awareness enabling you to spot the magic of synchronicity.

4. Follow your gut feeling and innate knowing.
If there's one thing my mum taught me from a young age, it's to trust your gut instinct - it will never let you down! If you receive a sign, and the action feels right to take, don't hesitate. If it doesn't feel right, listen to it! We all have an innate knowing, an inner guidance. You may receive a sign but it just doesn't align with

what you want. That's perfectly fine and might be a sign for you to realise it's not what you want. Listen to your gut feeling.

5. Ask questions.
If you are at a crossroads, or just not sure what direction to take, ask! Ask The Universe for a sign to guide you on the right path. Ask for clarity on what you should do. Your guidance can come in any form, so once you have asked your question, practise being mindful and aware of what is showing up. If you're looking for confirmation on something and you don't receive a sign, the lack of sign can in fact be a sign.

6. Surrender & release expectations of the outcome.
Once you have set your intention, create the space for magic to happen by releasing the expectation of the outcome. Remember the self-fulfilling prophecy of what you think about? When you attempt to control an outcome, the opposite happens. You attract whatever you focus on, so surrender and release the expectation. Let synchronicity show up. Go about your day and expect to receive guidance along the way.

7. Trust & take action.
If you want sizzling synchronicities to occur, you need to trust the inner guidance. If you feel like phoning someone, do it. If you feel like watching a particular movie, do it. If you feel like getting into nature, do it. Trust your intuition and take action. You never know what will show up from those initial instincts. It is the taking action upon receiving a sign that will lead you to the next sign. If you don't act, you can't receive the next breadcrumb on your trail to what you want. Trust that when you feel the need to do something, it may be leading you to something else.

Signs from The Universe

"There is no such thing as chance; and what seems to us merest accident springs from the deepest source of destiny."
~ Friedrich Schiller

Synchronicities can vary from person to person. It is a personal message to you from The Universe. Some common sizzling synchronicities are:

- Seeing repetitive numbers such as 111, 222, 444 in various forms such as on a clock, a date, a number plate, a phone number or a pattern such as 1234, 1212.
- Thinking of someone and running into them or them phoning you!
- Meeting someone who happens to have a clear message in what they say, do, or where they come from. Random interactions with people who don't know you are powerful ways to receive messages.
- Having opportunities appear when you least expect them (such as stumbling across the publishing company for this book!)
- Hearing a phrase or line of a song that causes you to stop and listen closer. It's like they're specifically talking to you!
- Having regular symbols show up whether as animals or inanimate objects (an infinity symbol or picture of something).
- Overhearing a conversation that triggers something inside you.

WHAT THEY THINK IS NOT MY BUSINESS

The list really can go on and on. Just remember, if it means something to you, it's more than likely a message personally for you. Open your eyes, open your heart, and most importantly act on the sign you are receiving. By taking action from this inspired state, you are showing The Universe you are ready for the next step!

ACTION

1. Quieten your mind.
   - Take five to ten minutes to sit still, let go of any thoughts or stresses presently going on in your world, focus on your breath and relax your body.
   - Listen to relaxing music or even a guided meditation (you can find many different guided meditations on YouTube) if your mind won't quieten.
   - If you find yourself thinking a thought, bring your focus back to your breath and listen to the music or meditation.

2. Set your intention. What guidance do you want to receive? What sign would you like to see? Once you set your intention, release the expectation of the outcome and trust you will receive what you ask for.

3. Journal afterwards about what came up for you. Did you see anything? Hear anything? Feel anything? What inspired thoughts came from this? If nothing came to you, that's ok!

SIZZLING SYNCHRONICITIES

Make this a regular practice. The more you do it, the better you get, and the clearer your mind will become to receive messages.

4. Take action when you do receive guidance. If your synchronicity is an affirmation that you are on the right path, great! Keep doing what you're doing. If you have an inspired thought, or idea, act on it immediately.

CHAPTER SUMMARY

- In every moment, you are gently being guided from a higher power.

- Synchronistic signs are unique and meaningful to the person to whom it is happening. What means something to one person, has no relevance to another.

- There are no coincidences in life. Everything happens at the right time, for a reason greater than any of us can understand.

- Not receiving a sign can indeed be a sign!

- Ask for a sign, release the expectation of it coming and wait for it to show up.

You have this vision of how you want your life to be, you're gently being guided and you're prepared to start moving forward. What if I told you there was a way to fast track your results? You're not going to want to skim through Chapter 9, where you will learn how easy it is to fast track everything you want.

CHAPTER 9

Fast Track Your Success

Is there really a way to fast track your success? I'm not here to give you false promises or sugar coat anything - but I can tell you there is a way to fast track everything that you want. However, let's be clear - you will not get away without taking action. You can wish, visualise and hope all you like but until you take real world action, you won't achieve anything. What I'm going to share with you in this chapter IS the answer to fast tracking results and ultimately your success, coupled with direct real-world action.

Knowing this piece of the success formula, changes everything. Back when I came across the movie The Secret, I was instantly cast into a world of positive thinking, goal setting and visualisation. I completely believed in the Law of Attraction and was taking massive action towards my goals. What I didn't know back then, was that was only part of the success formula. Since the movie, the Law of Attraction has been scientifically supported with quantum physics and proven physical changes occurring in the brain, as we have discussed previously. It's no longer esoteric, wishful thinking but it still misses the mark with giving the whole picture.

It is possible to fast track your success and learning this piece of the puzzle has had the greatest impact on my personal results. Of course, it's one thing to learn it and it's another to implement it. Are you ready to power up your results and get there faster, regardless of what other people think? Applying this is key to attracting more of what you want into your life - more money, more love, more passion, more time, more health, more, more, more.

Looking back over the past 20 or so years, while I did create great results, I can see how I possibly could have created better ones implementing this missing piece. Since learning this, it has changed everything. I'm only human, and of course I do slip back into "poor me" moments but, I am able to consciously bring myself out and swiftly change my emotional state, all from knowing the secret to fast tracking my success.

Setting goals, visualising and taking action are all parts of the success formula, except it's missing a key element. Continuing to leave this out is like leaving out the flour when baking a cake! You may take the action needed but without this, you just won't reach your true potential, or get the results you want. You may even experience self-sabotage and work against your goal.

So, are you ready to fast track your success?

The Missing Piece

Success in any area of your life begins with having a really clear picture of what it is you want to achieve. With this picture in mind, most people work with the formula:

Set a Goal + Take Action = Desired Results

However, it is missing a key component.

Being Your Future Self.

Every day we 'show up' a certain way. Some days it may be as the driven, passionate, positive person charging towards your goals, and other days it could be as a whinging, complaining, needy person who is moving away from your goals. Who you show up as and who you are BEING is the secret to fast tracking your progress.

The game changing question becomes not "What do I need to do?" but instead "Who do I need to BE?"

ACTION

Imagine yourself having achieved exactly what you want. Take yourself to that moment and make note of as much detail as possible. Where are you? What is surrounding you? What are you wearing? Who are you with? What are you holding? What can you hear? What are you saying? What can you smell?

> Next, think about the person you have *become* in this moment? Are you confident? Determined? Passionate? Humble? Joyous? Driven? Unstoppable? Abundant? Get really clear on the attributes this *future you* has in order to have achieved your desired outcome.
>
> Finally, the last piece is to describe how you're feeling. In this moment, how do you feel? What is the collective energy of this moment? Are there people surrounding you? What is their feeling? Do you feel calm, peaceful, proud, overwhelmed with gratitude, full of joy, or love, excited, blissful? Describe these feelings and emotions in as much detail as possible.
>
> THIS is your Future Self.

If you find this exercise challenging, another strategy to use can be to find someone who has achieved the success you are looking to create. What kind of person would create these outcomes? What must they believe - in themselves, in their results and in the world? What language do they use? Who do they surround themselves with? How do they dress? Act? What is their relationship with money? With their body? With their mind? By BEING this kind of person, you too can have access to the same results they do. This was certainly something I did in my early years of entrepreneurship. I thought of my mentor and inspiration, Jon, and imagined myself also as this successful charismatic, motivational person.

Your Lower Self vs Your Future Self

Now you have a clear description of your Future Self, it's time to bridge the gap and remove the disconnect of who you are NOW to this future version of you. I found this exercise so enlightening and transformative. I have always been driven and self-motivated however, before understanding this concept, I now realise I was strangling the life out of my desires and Future Self. I would grind it out, forcing outcomes, feeling stressed and anxious when it didn't go my way and, to be honest, I was highly critical and inauthentic towards myself, my actions and my lack of results. This internal fight would repel what I really wanted and I would feel overcome with fear that it wasn't ever going to happen. Do you think 'being' this way was attracting what I wanted or pushing my goals away? Of course, it continued to prevent everything I wanted from coming into my life.

It wasn't until I got the formula right, that things started to dramatically shift and my life turned around. My Future Self is an empowered, confident woman who allows The Universe to surprise her with delivering her needs and desires. She is an action taker, abundant and fluid in motion. She is completely present in this moment, while keeping her eyes firmly fixed on her goals. She is easy going, fun to be around, authentic and uplifts those with whom she connects. She is a big thinker, is humble and full of gratitude for what she has accomplished thus far. She is experienced, although remains a student 100% of the time. She is highly respected, and respectful to herself and others. She is calm, peaceful, poised and trusts The Universe. It's almost as if achieving her goals is easy and effortless. She knows the secret.

WHAT THEY THINK IS NOT MY BUSINESS

"Do something today that your future self will thank you for."
~ Sean Patrick Flanery

The person I was being before I did this exercise was not my Future Self. Very quickly, I realised I needed to fix my formula for success. My Lower Self was forcing things to happen. My Future (or Higher) Self is allowing things to happen. My Lower Self constantly battled internally. My Future Self is supportive, compassionate and confident in the outcome. My Lower Self put so much pressure on 'arriving' at the goal. My Future Self relishes in the journey and the process.

What is your disconnect? Recognise who you have been (up to this point) and who you need to be to move forward. At any point, we can choose who we are being. It is a conscious choice and can attract very quickly everything you want. The perfect partner, the perfect job, the perfect business, the perfect house, the perfect opportunity. You must be aligned with this future version of you to attract your desires now.

ACTION

Write a letter from your Future Self to your Present Self. What would they say? What insight would they share with you?

Getting the Formula Right

Most people live in a HAVE - DO - BE state. They believe they need to 'have' something, so they can 'do' something, which in turn will allow them to 'be' what they truly want.

Here are a few examples of how the formula is used <u>incorrectly</u>:

When I *have* enough money, I will start that business (*do*) and then I will *be* successful.

When I *have* lost that extra weight, I will join that fun run (*do*) and then I will *be* confident.

When I *have* met the right person, I will look after myself (*do*) and then I will *be* fulfilled.

When I *have* more time, I will *do* that course, and then I will *be* inspired to follow my heart.

When I *have* been promoted, I will save enough money to buy that home (*do*), and I will *be* financially secure.

When I *have* created financial success, I will write that book (*do*), and I will *be* a published author.

Can you see how this formula and the person you are being is 1) completely reliant on the having of the goal and 2) preventing you from attracting that which you desire by keeping you in victim mode? While you do not have what you want, you are blocking yourself from being your Future Self. It is very easy to start comparing yourself to those who are creating the results you desire from this method, as you may think, "If I had what that person has, then

WHAT THEY THINK IS NOT MY BUSINESS

I'd be as successful, happy or fit as they are." This is completely disempowering and from a mindset of lack.

Let's look at how things can be changed with reversing the recipe:

BE - DO - HAVE

I am a successful entrepreneur (*being*), starting my own business (*do*), which will allow me to *have* financial success to live my life how I choose.

I am confident in myself (*being*), joining in local fun runs, eating healthily (*do*), which supports my weight goals (*have*).

I am *being* an attractive potential partner, working on my personal happiness, fulfilment and contentment, taking care of my own emotional needs, and allowing myself to build on my confidence and independence (*doing*), which will attract my perfect partner (*have*).

I support and live my passion (*being*), by taking courses and educating myself so that I can build my business (*do*), giving me more choices and flexibility (*have*).

I am great with managing money (*being*), saving and planning my financial future (*do*) which will allow me to buy my dream home (*have*).

I am a creative writer (*being*), who can beautifully articulate information through words (*do*), for which I am handsomely compensated for (*have*).

These two different scenarios have very different energetic feelings. One comes from a mindset of lack, the other comes from a mindset of abundance. One will repel the outcome that is sought, the other will attract everything desired. If you took the same actions, you would get very different results with both scenarios.

You cannot be an unhealthy person, take the actions of a fit, active person and expect to get the results. It just doesn't work by law.

"You have to be before you can do, and do before you can have."
~ Zig Ziglar

Where have you fallen short of being your Future Self? The person that HAS achieved your goals. What skills, attributes or characteristics does your Future Self have that you can implement immediately? What would be a non-negotiable for your Future Self? What would they do differently to what you are doing now? What do you need to do to fully express this identity? Be that person from this point and then take Action.

Your life can shift very quickly just by changing this formula. In hindsight, there may be moments or opportunities that have passed you by because you were waiting to have more money, skills, time or love before being that Future Self. This is simply maintaining the gap between where you are now and where you want to be.

As the Dalai Lama said, *"We are human beings, not human doings."* Allow your life to take off in ways you could never imagine by getting the formula right.

WHAT THEY THINK IS NOT MY BUSINESS

Triggers for Your Lower Self

Trying to close the gap between where you are now and your Future Self, who has achieved everything you want, can be like a baby giraffe learning to walk. You may stumble here and there, slip down or even need to start all over again. This up-down journey is all part of the process of *becoming*. Rather than beat yourself up for thinking as your Lower Self, or responding in a manner your Lower Self would, acknowledge it and choose again. At any moment, you can choose who you are being.

Recognising triggers that cause your lower self to react will support you in the process. Such triggers can be people, situations, events, lack of sleep, stress, anxiety, just to name a few. What we want to do here is recognise what triggers you to act, behave or react in a manner of your Lower Self so you can consciously choose your surroundings, or develop tools to deal with the situation you are in so you can be your Future Self as much as possible.

When I started my online business, I went into action immediately. I wrote to do lists, researched everything I could, set some huge audacious goals and literally felt like rubber was burning under my feet. However initially, I didn't go very far. While my Future Self was standing in the wings waiting for me, my Lower Self was grinding it out, making everything harder than it needed to be - literally. I had a limiting belief that for anything to be worthwhile, I had to almost kill myself to achieve it.

I realised I had an ingrained belief from when I was 14 years old that was infiltrating my ability to be my Future Self. This belief came from a comment a family friend made in reference to me as a "little Aussie Battler". Although I can recognise this person meant it as a compliment, it had a negative impact on how I came to view success and what it took to create it. As I grew up, I developed a belief that life, work, and being successful was a battle. When I decided very early on in my working life that I wanted to be an entrepreneur and be financially and personally successful, I didn't realise it would take me almost two decades to discover this underlying belief I held onto that it had to be a battle. Talk about 'being' my Lower Self! In hindsight, I can recognise how I had subconsciously made everything a 'battle' - from relationships, to having children, to business success.

Yep, it wasn't until I recognised the Lower Self mindset I had that I was then able to switch things up, align with my Future Self and change my method.

Once I grasped this concept within my business and aligned with my Future Self, I started being the leader - thinking like a leader, behaving like a leader - and I started attracting the perfect clients to my business. It wasn't about being inauthentic, but about embodying the desired states of being a person who has accomplished what I wanted. As my Future Self, I had created the results I wanted - even before my first client came along. When in my Lower Self state, grinding it out, I was stuck in the present disempowered position and was not where I wanted to be. Once I started *being* the leader that my Future Self was - clients or no clients - my business, and life boomed.

When I'm looking to make a significant change in my life, I look to what my Future Self would say or do from where I'm at. From this point, I can make an action plan. When I feel myself starting to slip back to my Lower Self, I simply go back asking, "What would my Future Self do?" Triggers to pull you back can happen at any moment, don't dwell on it when it happens. Just dust yourself off, *get out of your own way* and choose who you are being again.

WHAT THEY THINK IS NOT MY BUSINESS

"We always have a choice: to listen to our lower self and indulge or to listen to our higher self and improve."
~ Gaur Gopal Das

Supercharge Your Future Self State

So, you've got all the ingredients for your formula for success. This is where things begin to heat up. As we covered in Chapter 4, your emotional state is your indicator of your mindset. You simply cannot take positive action being in a negative emotional state. The same applies with being your Future Self. There must be a positive emotional charge attached for this component of the formula to work.

When my Lower Self was forcing things to happen by grinding it out, I stank of desperation and fear. Despite my outward positive nature, what I was really projecting, was in fact, keeping everything I wanted at a distance. When I realised this (after a good honest look at myself), I turned those feelings behind what I doing into those of my Future Self - excitement, knowing and joy. Instantly, my Future Self took over and every action I took had a different intention and meaning behind it. The same actions can be taken but the intention behind them can be very different, with different emotions.

What feelings do you attach to your Future Self? How do you feel when you imagine yourself achieving your goal? What emotions come up for you? Are you feeling proud of yourself? Abundant? Assured? Secure? Blissful? Ecstatic? Peaceful? Are these feelings going to *supercharge* you into who you are being? Move forward being your Future Self with these empowering emotions and just watch what happens.

FAST TRACK YOUR SUCCESS

We all have the ability to show up in any state of being at any time. It is not only when goals are met or things work out as we want. Remember who you are being, supercharged with positive emotions, that creates the intention behind what we do and therefore affects the results we desire.

CHAPTER SUMMARY

- Uncovering the missing piece of the success formula will fast track your success.

- Who you are BEING changes the intention behind your actions.

- Bridge the gap between your Lower Self and your Future Self and you become a magnet to what you desire.

- Get the formula right and come from an abundance mindset - Be the person, then take the Action (Do), in order to Have your ideal life.

- Supercharge your Future Self state by attaching positive emotion to it.

It's so exciting to be on this journey with you as you create the life of your dreams. The path to getting there is never a straight one (wouldn't it be great if it was?!) In Chapter 10, we build your ultimate arsenal, preparing you for any challenge you may face along the way!

CHAPTER 10

Your Ultimate Arsenal

"Before anything else, preparation is the key to success."
~ Alexander Graham Bell

My husband, Kevin, and I recently purchased a Nissan Navara (his pride and joy!) to start going on 4WD adventures and family camping getaways. I'm not really a camping girl but I'm open to new experiences with family and friends. Before we even got the car, he was buying all these things we were going to need - tents, canopies, portable stove, car fridge, oh the list goes on. He thought of every possible item we would need to be comfortable (and probably for me to enjoy it!). I must say that although I did have a few eye roll moments during his spending spree, I am really glad he prepared us as much as he did.

WHAT THEY THINK IS NOT MY BUSINESS

I mean, could you imagine if we rocked up to a camp site and didn't have a tent? Sure, it might be fun for our girls (not so for me!), but what if it was raining? Not fun at all.

The same principle applies with preparing and filling your own toolbox for your journey towards your goals and in life. As the saying goes, "Proper Preparation Prevents Piss Poor Performance" (aka "The 6P's"). Equipping yourself with tools to see your goals through to the end is like packing the essentials for the camping trip. Being properly prepared is giving yourself the best possible chance of success.

Not having a box of tools to help you along the way can lead to the very first hurdle taking you out of the game. It will feel like a struggle and as if it's just not meant to be. If there's one thing for certain, it's that the journey to success and happiness will not be a straight one, so expect challenges and be prepared to handle them promptly. Arming yourself for success will also make the journey enjoyable! You'll feel like Lara Croft ready for that next encounter, ready to knock obstacles out of your way! You will be unstoppable.

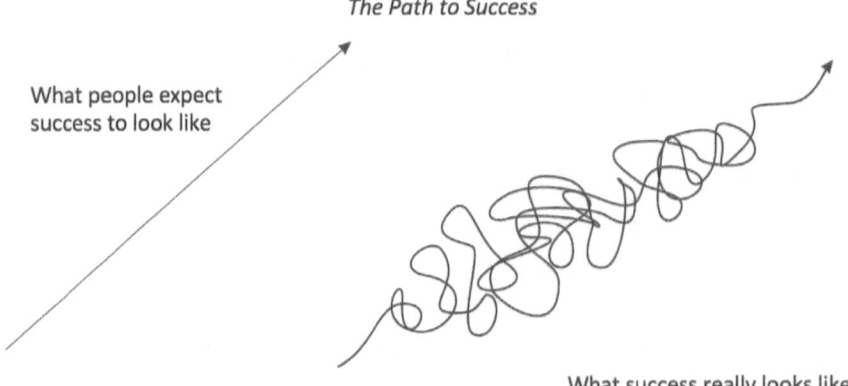

The Path to Success

What people expect success to look like

What success really looks like

A few years ago, I joined a fundraiser walk with a group of friends. It was 30 kilometres of beach, road and bush terrain. I had never participated in anything like this before and did not know what to expect. I had been physically active for over 20 years and thought, "How hard can it be?" Kev thought I was insane, knowing that I didn't realise what I had gotten myself into. Leading up to the walk, I did no extra or specific training, nor did I really even prepare for, or research, the route or terrain. I mean, it was just a walk, right?

Oh boy, just a 'walk' couldn't be further from the truth. I have never experienced such pain before in my life. I was used to throwing weights around, doing road running and teaching group fitness classes - not speed walking on uneven ground, through varying landscapes for six and a half hours. Kev and our girls met us along the way with water and snacks and each time I saw him, the urge to tell him he was right and ask him to take me home, got stronger. I would not admit it to my friends - or him at the time - but I was in a world of pain. I did finish that horrendous walk (and cried at the finish line) and can now see in hindsight that my lack of preparation made it all the more painful.

Preparing for The Unknown

Your journey to whatever you desire doesn't need to be as painful as that 30 kilometres was for me. You just need to be prepared for what possibly may come your way in the process. You're probably wondering how you can prepare for unknown obstacles? Good question. We never know what is really going to pop up along the way, we can just do our best to prepare.

Every person and situation will require a different set of tools. There are the practical and technical tools you will need to achieve your goal. For example, if you want to be an online marketer, you will need to learn how to write ads, search effective platforms on which to market on, know who to market to, as well as the use of keywords and Search Engine Optimisation. The practical and technical skills you will need to learn will be specific to the goal you have set. That's not the toolbox I'm talking about here.

What I'm talking about are more individualised tools to maintain your momentum in taking the action required to achieve what you desire. I mentioned that it felt like I hit a brick wall when I started my online business and was faced with negative comments from family and friends about 'this sort of business'. Ironic that I titled this book, "What They Think Is Not My Business", right? If my goal of being a successful online entrepreneur wasn't strong enough, and if I didn't have the tools to deal with these comments, I may have stopped before I even got started. How devastating that would have been - for my own vision as well as my customers, clients and the friends I have made along the way.

Arming yourself with tools to help you in your journey will keep you on track when things get a little hazy. You will be able to maintain your high vibration enabling you to continue to attract that which you want, even in the midst of what may be chaos. So, let's start building your very own toolbox - it will be different to mine and different to anyone else's. Pick what resonates with you and leave the rest. You may even find this is a chapter you come back to when you need a little pick me up!

Self-Care
This has to be at the top of the list. For me - being a mum, wife, entrepreneur, boss, athlete, friend, daughter, sister, cook, cleaner, taxi driver - life can be hectic to say the least! It is essential that you look after yourself, so you have the energy, time and ability to

YOUR ULTIMATE ARSENAL

give to others, as well as your goals. I have experienced periods of burn out before when I have neglected myself and it's not fun. You literally have nothing left to give.

This can be challenging for some mothers (and fathers), as they devote their life to their family. When I finally became a mum (after unsuccessful IVF rounds and a miscarriage), my whole world revolved around my baby. It wasn't until later that I realised I was able to be a *better* mum, by taking time out for myself. Don't get me wrong, in the beginning I struggled with guilt when doing something just for myself. However, I have witnessed the positive effects on my girls over the years by taking time out. I am definitely more patient, giving, open, energised and balanced by doing so.

The same principle can be applied to your goals and life. If you are constantly putting in sweat and tears, spending every waking minute working towards your vision without taking time out for yourself, you will crash and burn. Fast. Also, to be honest, you won't be doing your best work. For you to be functioning at your peak, self-care must be a number one priority.

Fill your cup! Ways I fill my cup include going for walks along the beach or lake, taking bubble baths, having a coffee catch up with my bestie, playing with my fur baby, doing my favourite exercise class, having a wine and phoning a friend for a chat, treating myself to a massage, manicure or pedicure, going shopping (even window shopping), watching a movie, reading a book, or even going on a mini getaway with the ladies of my family!

Self-care is about doing what fills your cup - even if that means doing nothing (like meditating). It's about coming back to your work, or family, feeling refreshed and re-energised. Giving yourself permission to take time out for you, will also give you more clarity on your vision and goal. The more you have in your cup, the more you have to give.

> *"Self-care is giving the world the best of you, instead of what's left of you."*
> **~ Katie Reed**

Do Something That You Love

What fills your heart with joy? It might be horse riding, knitting, doing a jigsaw puzzle, cooking or reading. Whatever the activity, it is something that brings joy to your heart. When you are feeling joy and 'light', you will attract joyful, happy things to your life.

This one can be particularly useful when you are feeling 'stuck' on something. Perhaps you have been working on a project and just can't seem to move through a challenge. Feeling heavy in your mind and heart isn't a good place to be when you're trying to figure something out. Doing something that you love will return you to a calm and happy state, which will not only make you feel better, but will also allow you to see challenges through different eyes.

Balance and Harmony

Spread your activities out across a number of things. If you put all your eggs in one basket, you will run the risk of being out of balance and harmony in your life. Next to my family, business is absolutely my number one priority; however, I don't let it be the ONLY thing I'm focused on. Making my feeling of success, happiness or confidence dependent on one thing (my business), is way too much pressure to make things work. In the beginning, I was guilty of this and I let other aspects or interests fall to the side. In doing this, guess what happened? Did my business boom because that's where all my focus went? Nope. The opposite occurred. It was as if I had hit the pause button. It was not good for my energy, or the level at which I was vibrating. I'm pretty sure at the time, my potential clients could smell that sense of desperation through the phone.

The ongoing success of my business remains my primary goal however, I have spread my interests across a number of areas. Writing this book was one of them! Maintaining a regular exercise program is another. What can you do to bring more balance and harmony into your life? Are there smaller goals on which you can focus some time? Absolutely have your main goal (and keep that main thing, the main thing!) but create smaller interests, or mini goals, so when you are in need of balance, you can take time in another area. Avoid the risk of putting all your eggs in one basket.

Connect with Others

As social beings, we are genetically designed to seek connections with others. It is both soul soothing and calming. Connecting with others can be with those you love, but it can also be with those who have created the level of success you desire.

> *"I love connecting with people who have been through the fire and come out stronger and wiser. Using their experiences to inspire and empower others. Those are my people."*
> **~ Steve Maraboli**

When you're working on achieving your goal, there may be times where you question whether you can do it. Connecting with others who have walked the walk, have overcome hurdles and achieved success, will drive and push you forward. This connection can be in person, or it may be virtually. You may listen to a podcast, join a support group, or even reach out to someone you don't know but admire. Whether you personally know them or not really doesn't matter. Tony Robbins is someone I love to connect with - through his books, podcasts, or social media. I always feel inspired and have a deeper belief in myself after listening to him.

A huge bonus with the company I partner with is the community we have. I am continually influenced and inspired by connecting with others and hearing their stories, tribulations and triumphs. I have never personally known of a community of people who openly share their journeys, or who are so supportive and encouraging. Whenever I'm feeling uncertain or frazzled, connecting with others helps me turn these feelings around and get me back on track.

Who Do You Surround Yourself With?

You may have connections with others globally, but have a look at who you are surrounding yourself with the majority of the time. Do they lift you up or pull you down? As Jim Rohn says, "You are the average of the five people you spend the most time with." The people with whom who you spend the most time shape who you are. In preparing yourself for your success journey, having people who uplift, support and inspire you is essential. Think of the conversations you have with those around you. Are they positive and encouraging? Do they fill your soul and make you want to do better, be better and achieve more?

Who you surround yourself with has a direct impact on your attitude and motivation to move toward your goals. When the going gets tough, will they support you? Do they believe in you or will they give you a "I told you so" look at the first obstacle you face?

Three Types of People - Campers, Pullers, and Climbers

I first heard this interesting concept from Jon Mailer about 20 years ago, during one of his personal development courses, and it has stuck with me since. He explained three categories of people - Campers, Pullers and Climbers. Understanding this concept has helped me understand those I come into contact with, and therefore enables me to make effective choices around whom I surround myself with.

The Camper

A camper is someone who is very happy with where they are at in their life. They have worked consistently to get to a point where they are content and satisfied, and they are not really interested in aiming for more. They are not phased, and do not concern themselves with what other people are doing. They are happy for other's success, are comfortable and confident in themselves and their accomplishments. They are usually happy to go with the status quo and remain in a safe place, rarely taking risks.

The Puller

A puller is someone with a negative attitude, who is pessimistic and has a "can't do" attitude, with a closed minded view of the world. The puller will do what it takes to pull you back down to their level, if they perceive you as rising above them. They usually have not achieved much in their life, and they knock anyone who is trying to achieve anything more than mediocrity. The puller is dangerous to be around as they will suck the life out of your goal. Minimise, if not avoid, contact with the puller.

WHAT THEY THINK IS NOT MY BUSINESS

The Climber

A climber is going places. They never stop learning, they have a positive, can-do attitude and are looking for the next mountain to climb. The climber is a high achiever, and never gives up. They change course if needed, but are relentless in the pursuit of their goals. A climber is encouraging and optimistic towards others, and relishes in others' success as much as their own. They want to see others succeed and be happy and they will pull their tribe up to the top of the mountain to be with them.

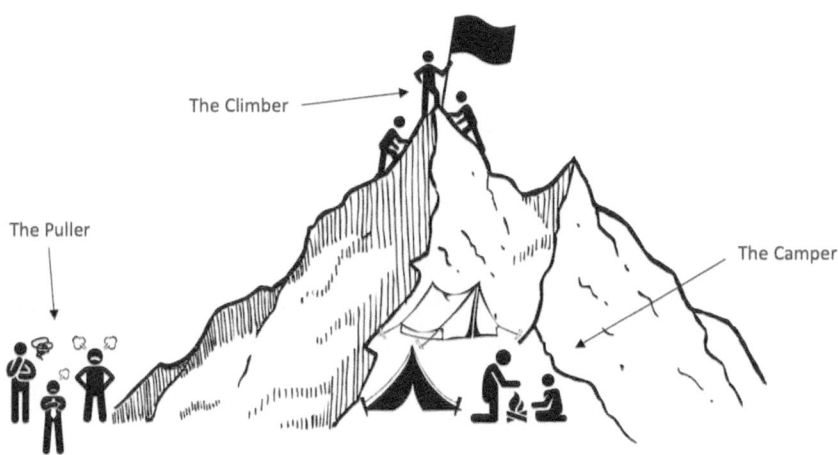

I have found understanding the three types of people especially important in times of need. When faced with a challenge, I have been able to draw on others' belief in me by surrounding myself with climbers. Imagine being vulnerable, trying to find a solution and being around a puller, or a camper. The puller will make you feel worse, as they infect you with their negativity. The camper is happy to go with the flow and probably won't have any words of encouragement, as they don't understand why you're even trying to achieve something. Whereas, the climber will inject enthusiasm, support and inspire you to keep going.

YOUR ULTIMATE ARSENAL

Having a strong support network directly around you not only strengthens your own belief, but also encourages you to strive to reach your goals. If you find that the ones you spend the most time with aren't supportive or positive, it may be time to find a new circle. When building your ultimate arsenal, having the right people around you is fundamental to your success and journey.

Radically Shifting Your Energy

This has to be one of my favourite tools to have in my toolkit! By now, you understand that like attracts like and while you're in a negative state, attracting that which you desire just won't happen. You're ready to change things up in your life and attract more of what you want, right? In order to do that, your energy (and therefore your vibration) needs to be at a high level. You simply cannot attract the perfect partner while you are feeling deflated, depressed or exhausted!

> *"As you think, you vibrate.*
> *As you vibrate, you attract."*
> **~ Abraham-Hicks**

There are so many ways to shift your vibration and raise it when you start to feel yourself spiral down. Not everything will work for you, but I encourage you to try them all at least once!

Cold showers. Yep, you read that right. Cold frigging showers. I first tried this in the *middle of winter*. It was suggested to me by a coach I had at the time, and I thought she was insane. But I gave it a go. Now it's a regular practice of mine! I usually have a

WHAT THEY THINK IS NOT MY BUSINESS

'normal' shower first, do my business and then for the last 30-60sec turn the hot water off completely (sorry, luke warm temperature does not count). Just before you get under the water, think of your goal and visualise yourself having achieved it. As you jump under the cold water, focus heavily on the achievement of your goal and stepping in as your Future Self. Allow the water to flow over you and embrace the feelings of your accomplishment. It is so rejuvenating, revitalising and stirs up your energy! Why limit this technique to the morning or evening time? Cold showers in the middle of the day also are a great way to shift stubborn thought patterns!

Elastic band snap. This technique is primarily used for literally snapping yourself out of negative thought pattern. If negative thoughts or self-limiting beliefs are a battle you have, try this trick. Simply wear an elastic band on your wrist. Anytime you have a thought that is negative or limits you such as, "I can't do this" or "I'll never do it", snap the elastic on your wrist. It will literally shock that thought away. Instantly replace the thought with a positive, empowering one and feel your stinking thinking disappear. I used this a lot in my early days when I couldn't get a handle on my thoughts.

Shouting "NO" or "STOP". Be mindful where you are when using this one! Obviously if you are in an office full of people, or in the middle of a shopping centre, this technique may not be the best one to use at the time. If the situation permits, and you can't stop yourself from feeling doubt or fear, shouting "NO" or "STOP" as loud as you can is effective. It's about breaking the neural connection in the brain, interrupting the negative thought process and then replacing it with a positive one. I've even done this in the mirror looking at myself square in the eyes to get myself back on track.

YOUR ULTIMATE ARSENAL

Dance party. Turn. The. Music. UP. Have your own little dance party, whether it's at home or in the car. If you need an instant pick me up to shift your energy, get dancing and moving! I honestly feel tingles throughout my entire body when I do this. It's like energy is surging and firing through every fibre of my being. Talk about a vibrational shift! Put your favourite song on and just go for it. Feel the lift from your toes to the top of your head. When you're electrified with energy from your own dance party, you will be a powerful magnet, drawing to you exactly what you desire.

Get in nature. Connecting with Mother Nature is known to reduce stress and anxiety, improve blood pressure, breathing, and overall physical well-being. Not surprisingly, when we connect with nature, we are essentially grounding ourselves and ridding ourselves of the chaos of daily life. Disconnecting and appreciating the beauty of nature supports our mental and emotional state, while raising our vibration and energy. When you are feeling an overload and disconnect, try going for a bush walk or visit the beach. Take in the fresh air, feel the sun on your skin, smell the ocean or the trees, feel the sand between your toes or listen to the rustle of the leaves. Connect with the vibration of nature and feel your own vibration lift.

Exercise. Get the blood flowing to shift that energy. Back in my personal training days, I would hear, "I'm so tired, I don't feel like exercising." Yet every time we completed the session, my clients would comment on how energised they felt! It's a misconception that you need energy to exercise. Exercise actually gives you energy! If you're feeling stuck or trapped in a downward spiral, move your body! Go for a walk or run, go the gym, do yoga, go for a swim - just move your body. Literally move that energetic state right out of your body, and replace it with feeling of invigoration and endorphins - the good feeling hormones.

WHAT THEY THINK IS NOT MY BUSINESS

Meditate. Forcing a solution to appear when faced with an obstacle or to achieve a certain outcome, simply will not work. Going within, quietening the mind and connecting with The Universe can help you see things in a different light, or to feel an intuitive pull. It took me a while to master this practice, and I still have days where my mind just won't quieten. It surely can shift your vibration, the more you practise it. My hot tip here is if you get an idea, or feel a strong urge to do something after meditating, act on it promptly!

Personal Development. This one is a daily tool, for your way of thinking up to this point has gotten you to where you are now. In order to progress, or go to the next level, you have to change your thinking. Remain a student and be open to discovering yourself during the journey. Your outer world is a reflection of what's going on in your inner world, so when the road gets bumpy on your journey, think, "What do I need to learn about this and about myself?" My go to are audiobooks, books, podcasts or online courses (such as the ones our company has). Experiencing breakthroughs and ah-ha moments will lift your vibration and increase your energy.

Journal. If you face a difficult time in your journey, rather than letting the situation swirl around inside you, get it out on paper. It can help you see things more clearly, and also removes any feelings of negativity that are pulling down your vibration. You might use this tool after meditating when your thoughts are aligned with your goal. The idea of journaling is to dump your thoughts out of your head to make space for new insight. Definitely a go to that can shift things up and get out of your head that which is holding you down. A great way to make sure your vibration stays high.

ACTION

BUILD YOUR OWN ARSENAL

It's time to build your ultimate arsenal! Try each of the ones I've recommended and you may also find new ones. What works for me won't necessarily work for you, so build your own ultimate arsenal to draw on, when needed throughout your journey.

You may recognise your own self-limiting behaviours and resonate with some of the aforementioned strategies that will enable you to arm yourself accordingly. For example, you may be a former 'workaholic' and a useful tool to address this may be to set an alarm for you to stop work, physically get up and go for a walk outside. Some techniques may work sometimes and at other times they won't. The magic is in the commitment to the application - if one doesn't work, move to the next.

"Confidence comes from being prepared."
~ John Wooden

CHAPTER SUMMARY

- The success of anything relies on being properly prepared!

- Creating a toolkit of techniques to keep your vibration up is essential to continually attracting what you desire.

- Fill your cup up first, so you have more to give others.

- Radically shift your energy to raise your vibration through dance, music, cold showers, surrounding yourself with climbers and other techniques.

- Building your own personalised arsenal will prepare you for the challenges and obstacles you may face along the way.

There is one single human emotion that has the power to transform everything. You can feel this emotion and use it instantly at any given moment. Feeling into this emotion will power up your results immediately. What is it? Find out in Chapter 11!

CHAPTER 11

Power Up Your Results

"A grateful heart is a magnet for miracles."
~ Unknown

There is one human emotion that has the power to transform and increase your results over all other emotions. **Gratitude**. Understanding its power is fundamental to achieving the life you truly desire, and being a magnet in the process. This is so crucial, not only for achieving goals, but also your overall happiness. No matter your starting point, you can power up your results and start attracting everything you truly want through the use of Gratitude.

I've never met anyone who didn't want to improve their life in one way or another. A better job. Better business results. Better relationships. Better health. Better financial situations. However, searching and yearning for something *better* can leave us feeling

WHAT THEY THINK IS NOT MY BUSINESS

a sense of lack when we are yet to have it. This is particularly prominent in high achievers, as they go for more and can be derailed when they don't "see" results, they only see what they have yet to achieve. Coming from the position of lack will repel the very result we are trying to achieve, along with bringing a heavy heart. A lack of Gratitude will lead to feelings of resentment. Definitely not setting the scene for your dreams to come true, right?

I never really understood the principle of, "It's not the outcome of the goal that is most important but the person you become along the way" until I started practising Gratitude. In my 20s, I found myself putting too much attention on what I wanted to create, rather than taking a moment to appreciate where I was, and what I had accomplished. It was like I was living for the future, rather than in the present. These days, life is very different and consequently, so are my results. I definitely attribute this to Gratitude.

> *"Acknowledging the good that you already have is the foundation for all abundance."*
> **~ Ekhart Tolle**

Gratitude is one of the most powerful emotions. Practicing Gratitude leads to many health benefits, not only do you transform your energy to get more of what you want, but your overall physical, emotional and mental state improves. Practising Gratitude brings you to a positive emotional state, improves your health, enables you to appreciate good experiences, connects you to something greater, helps you deal with adversity and contributes to building strong relationships.

Developing an Attitude of Gratitude

Developing an attitude of Gratitude is a practice, especially in the pursuit of changing your life. It is taking a moment to appreciate the present, the past, as well as what is to come. Gratitude is a choice. It is pausing and acknowledging all the good things in our lives and what is surrounding us. It is about opening and expanding your heart which allows more moments for which to be grateful to appear!

Appreciating this moment, and all it has to offer, opens your heart and is an important element in the Law of Attraction. As we feel a deep sense of Gratitude, we are attracting more of what we can feel grateful for! The universal Law of Attraction states we will attract that which we think about and focus on. There is always something that we can be thankful for, even in moments of despair or stress. It could be feeling the warmth of the sun, or hearing the birds chirping in the morning. It could be a memory, or even the smile of a stranger. Hearing a song, receiving a hug from a loved one, having an opportunity or an idea present itself. However big or small, feel your Gratitude, find the greatness in the moment, and you will attract more to be grateful for.

The moment you shift from a place of lack and negativity to abundance, love and appreciation brings immediate changes and effects to your being and state. Your brain becomes more harmonised and balanced, your heart stabilises and beats in a more even rhythm, there are multiple biochemical changes, such as increased levels of dopamine and serotonin triggering a positive and 'feel good' emotional state of being. The impact gratitude has on your physical body alone is positive and supports your journey to achieving your new life.

WHAT THEY THINK IS NOT MY BUSINESS

"Be thankful for what you have, you'll end up having more. If you concentrate on what you don't have, you will never ever have enough."
– Oprah Winfrey

11 Ways to Practise Daily Gratitude

Keep a Gratitude Journal. Keeping a daily journal of all the things for which you're grateful for will have remarkable effects on your emotional state. It doesn't have to be a long process. Simply write down 5 things you're grateful for that day and 5 things you're grateful for that are coming. Feel into what it is you're grateful for in the moment - a fresh day ahead, a good night's sleep, morning coffee or tea. You simply cannot focus on the long list of to do's for the day, or a crappy night's sleep when you're journaling about the positive aspects of now and what you're looking forward to.

Keeping a Gratitude journal is also a great tool to be able to reflect back on the positive emotions and moments. Find what works best for you - listing in bullet points your blessings or writing in detail what you are grateful for.

Doing Random Acts of Kindness (RAK). There's nothing like doing something completely at random for someone else - with no expectation of anything in return. Just seeing (or hearing) their Gratitude makes me feel so grateful to have been able to give them that experience. Some examples of RAK's are leaving scratchies on people's cars, giving flowers to strangers in the shops, putting someone else's equipment away at the gym, offering to be the designated driver, paying for someone's coffee, nails, lunch, complimenting a stranger, donating to charity, volunteering at the local retirement or nursing home, scratching your pet's head for 15 minutes…the list really can go on and on. When you give without expectation, the effect is really incredible on both you, the giver, and also the person receiving.

Sending a Card of Appreciation and Thanks. Send someone a card letting them know how grateful you are for having them in your life! My friend, Tracey, is awesome at this. She has been sending cards for over ten years (to different people of course!), and it's incredible the impact she has on others. Letting someone know you are thankful for them, for what they did or just appreciating a quality they have, has a lasting effect on their state of mind and is so good for your own.

Nurturing a Friendship. Being grateful for a work colleague or acquaintance could lead to a friendship and building a support network. If nothing else, by being thankful and acknowledging this person, you will feel good and leave them feeling great.

Being Present and Mindful. This may need to be a conscious act if you are someone who rushes through each moment of the day. Stop and take note of what you are doing, where you are, and mindfully practise Gratitude for this moment. I love doing this on my walks, or at my girls' sporting events. I even consciously practise Gratitude in the middle of a movie I'm watching with my hubby. Being present grounds you in the moment, lifts your energy and emotions and feels awesome.

Smile More. When I was a little girl, my mum had a sign in our kitchen that read, "Smile. It makes people wonder what you've been up to." I love this! Unfortunately, there are a lot of people that just go about their days like groundhog day, acting on autopilot and going through the motions. Imagine getting your morning coffee and the impact you have on the barista by connecting through your eyes and smile. Smiling is contagious and just smiling more will positively impact you and others.

Compliment Someone. Genuine compliments are uplifting and magnetising. You are in essence telling someone what you like about them (and what you are grateful for). True Gratitude doesn't leave you feeling like you owe other people something - complimenting someone leaves you both feeling good and creates a cycle of happiness.

Meditation. Practising Gratitude meditation is a great way to connect with all things that make your soul happy. You can find many Gratitude meditations on the internet. If you find it challenging to quiet the mind, find a guided meditation that works for you. Here is a simple example of a Gratitude meditation practice.

- In a quiet place, get into a comfortable seated position.
- Relax and close your eyes.
- Focus on your breath, take ten deep breaths in through your nose, out through your mouth. As you exhale, relax your mind and body a little more with each breath.
- When you feel relaxed and ready, ask yourself, "What am I really grateful for?"
- Reflect on what comes up for you and expand on this positive experience.
- Feel any overall energy and body sensations as you recount your memory.
- Hold that thought and feeling as long as you like and allow your mind to drift to other things you are grateful for.

POWER UP YOUR RESULTS

"Gratitude opens the door to the power, the creativity, and the wisdom of The Universe."
~ Deepak Chopra

Acknowledge Your Own Strengths. This can be a tricky one for some, but trust me, this is particularly empowering. Either verbally speak what it is you are grateful for about yourself, what you love the most about being you, or write yourself a letter. We can become critical of ourselves, so take the time to focus on your strengths, what you can offer and what you truly love about yourself.

Say Thank You Often. Show your appreciation and gratitude to others, whether it's a customer you serve or someone serving you. Telling someone, "Thank you" is particularly soul filling. You never know how their day is going and your Gratitude can change everything for them, plus attracting to you more things for which to be grateful.

Reflect on Your Day. Each night before you go to sleep, reflect on at least one experience you encountered throughout the day for which you are thankful. Being grateful for what happened throughout your day is a beautiful way to fall asleep. Imagine the impact this has on your energy, subconscious and vibration!

As you build your game plan for achieving what you want the most, how you want to live your life and create the reality you desire, Gratitude will power up your results and get you there faster. You will notice more things come into your life to be grateful for, as well as just how rich and abundant your life already is. As you seize these moments of Gratitude, you will notice that you are no longer bothered by the small things that just don't count. You will be able to focus on the bigger picture and the important actions to take. As you are grateful for what you have already, while holding the picture of what you want, you are in an abundant mindset and will attract more of the good stuff.

ACTION

Start a daily Gratitude practice! Find what works for you - morning, evening or during the day. Begin to look at the abundance that surrounds you and feel thankful for what you do have *in this moment.*

What are you grateful for already in your life? What positivity can you find from your journey so far? The ups and downs all have a place. Discover what you are grateful for *from your past.*

What are you grateful for *that is coming?* What is it that you are excited for and feel like you already have, that is yet to come?

CHAPTER SUMMARY

- You cannot attract more into your life without feeling Gratitude for what you already have.

- Gratitude greatly supports and optimises your physical, mental and emotional health.

- Having an attitude of Gratitude is having a mindset of abundance, allowing a flow of more things for which to be grateful to come into your life.

- Gratitude strengthens relationships, and grounds us to the present moment.

- Make practising Gratitude a daily practice and feel its transformative power!

It's Game Day. This is where you step onto the field and take charge. You can wish and visualise all day long but without an actual game plan, nothing will change. What you do from this point on is going to make the difference. In Chapter 12, we pull it altogether and devise our game plan.

CHAPTER 12

Effective Kickass Action

"A goal without a plan is just a wish."
~ Antoine de Saint-Exupéry

So, you have the blueprint of everything you want, your vision of your ideal future and how you want to live. You have shifted your mindset to that of a winner, you are vibrating at the level of what you want, you are being your Future Self. You have your toolkit and you are armed for what may come along the way. You have a heart full of gratitude and you are attracting more for which to be grateful....

Now, what? It's action time.

You can wish all you like, write your affirmations and work on overcoming self-limiting beliefs, but if you don't take real-world action, you simply will not create the life you desire. There is no getting out of taking concrete, physical, consistent action towards what you want. No matter how badly you want something - to find the love of your life, become a successful entrepreneur or buy that dream home - without doing the work required, it will simply fail to come true.

Everything you have worked on to this point has prepared you for what you must now physically do. As Dean Graziosi says, "*A plan is the backbone of a goal*". Without a plan, your goal loses its spine and becomes nothing more than a wish. The action plan needs to be laid out, and most importantly, acted upon. No one is going to swoop in and do it for you. This is your moment. The time to create the change you want in your life, to live the life you have imagined is NOW. It will become your reality, with an effective kickass action plan.

"Action is the foundation key to all success."
~ Pablo Picasso

Without action, your goal will remain a dream. An unrealised wish. Your life will continue as it is, and unfortunately, you will remain at the mercy of others and outside forces. In order for you to produce real tangible results, you must take actionable steps.

Massive Consistent Action

As the saying goes, "Rome wasn't built in a day", and the same goes for any big achievement. Success will not happen with one action taken once for one day. Only deliberate action steps,

EFFECTIVE KICKASS ACTION

taken consistently over time, will bring about your desired results. You honestly wouldn't go to the gym once, and expect to walk out looking like an Aphrodite, would you? You can't expect to try something once - or even multiple times - and have it change your life completely. Success is a marathon - not a sprint. When you want something badly enough, you will do what it takes - for as long as it takes - to make it a reality. It will take time and there will be periods where nothing seems to be happening. Just keep going and hold on for the ride! Knowing what you want, and creating a path to get there takes time. Success doesn't happen overnight, and if you stay consistent in your actions, it will become your reality.

The only way I have been able to achieve a ranking of number one in the world is by consistent action. Imagine if I had started martial arts with this goal but trained haphazardly, with no real aim or purpose? Would I be the highest ranked female in the world? I can 100% say no. This goal would never have been achieved without consistent action taken over time.

The thing is, those who are willing to do what it takes, will achieve their outcome. Every time. Those who allow others to influence their thoughts and behaviour will never get there. Every time you come up with an excuse, you're talking yourself out of it. Taking action is about getting outside of your comfort zone and backing yourself. Time and time again.

Think of a snow ball. It may start incredibly small at the top of the mountain but as it rolls, and gets bigger, it builds both momentum and speed. The same principle applies to your consistent action. The more action you take and the longer you take it, the greater your momentum towards your goals and the sooner you will achieve them. If you are serious about creating your ideal life, the sooner you start taking consistent action towards it, the better.

WHAT THEY THINK IS NOT MY BUSINESS

No matter how big or small the action steps are, the key here is to always be moving towards your goal. In fact, the smaller the steps, performed consistently, the more rewarding the end result. As long as you are inching towards what you want, and creating momentum along the way, you will arrive at your destination. Keep going until you get what you want.

> *"If you can't fly then **run**, if you can't **run** then **walk**, if you can't **walk** then **crawl**, but whatever you do you have to keep moving forward."*
> **~ Martin Luther King, Jr.**

The Personal Development industry was valued at a whopping $39.99 Billion in 2020 and is expected to reach $56.66 Billion by 2027 (Grand View Research, 2020). This highlights how much people globally are wanting to better themselves and their lives. We know most New Year's resolutions are forgotten by 1st February. So, what percentage of people actually achieve their goals? Research suggests that only 10% of people accomplish their goals, meaning an incredible 90% of people don't. The question then is, what do the 10% of people do that the majority of others don't do? Simple, they have an action plan and they work their plan every day.

How Do You Eat an Elephant?

Desmond Tutu once wisely said that *"there is only one way to eat an elephant: a bite at a time."* Of course, none of us are actually going to eat an elephant, but the analogy is brilliant when working out how to achieve a massive goal, and to completely change your life. Simply, one step at a time.

EFFECTIVE KICKASS ACTION

Now you're definitely going to have to take more than one action step, but you get the picture. There will be multiple steps needed, simultaneously, or separately, in your journey. When looking at your 'big scary goal', break it down into milestones, or mini goals, that when accomplished add up to your main goal. These might be monthly steps, which can then be further broken down into weekly or daily actions. The key is to be continuously moving forward, however seemingly small the step may be. All these little steps accumulate over time and create habits that will support the outcome you are seeking.

> *"Procrastination is opportunity's assassin."*
> **~ Victor Kiam**

Sometimes, the goal is so big and your timeline may be so far into the future that most people hold off on taking any action until it's too late, and then give up. They may have all the intentions of getting started tomorrow, but unfortunately tomorrow never comes. They procrastinate and, as time goes by, their motivation drops, as does their commitment to achieving their goal. Having a plan, and working on the plan every day, will determine your success. Don't delay until tomorrow what can be done today.

Bite Size Chunks

What is it going to take to achieve your outcome? Keep it simple, and break it down to a set of smaller milestones that can be achieved along the way. Ask yourself, what needs to happen for that goal to be realised?

WHAT THEY THINK IS NOT MY BUSINESS

Start from the end and work your way backwards. With the end in mind, set milestones, that when all achieved, add up to the main goal. The end goal won't seem so overwhelming or unattainable when you break it down. Most goals will have three to five milestones to reach in order for the big goal to be achieved.

Once you have these milestones, it's time to break them down further into actionable steps. These can be daily or weekly habits that need to be completed, or they can be specific steps required to move you onto the next milestone. The key here is these steps are baby steps to your milestones. You will also want to assign a deadline to each of these action steps.

> *"Great things are done by a series of small things brought together."*
> **~ Vincent Van Gogh**

Ok, let's go through a few examples of how to break down a big scary goal into bite size chunks! I have created an Action Planner to help you break things down and help with your planning. You can download a blank template at www.jaimelaing.com/bonus.

Reminder: Establishing a strong **why** for your goal is absolutely essential to following through on your action steps. Be 100% clear and committed on how achieving this goal is going to better your life and those around you.

EFFECTIVE KICKASS ACTION

Example 1. Start an Online Business

My Big Goal	My goal is to start and build an online business earning over $100,000 per year
My Why:	I want to be doing something that I'm passionate about and helping others create a life they love. Earning over a 6 figure income will allow me to work from anywhere autonomously and be a positive role model to my children.

Milestones

Milestones		Deadline
1. Establish a business		22nd February
2. Build presence online		25th March
3. Generate inquiries		19th April
4. First Sale		30th May
5. $10K month income consistently		11th November

Milestones

1. Establish a business	✓	2. Build presence online	✓	3. Generate Inquiries	✓	4. First Sale	✓	5. $10K monthly income	✓
Action Steps		**Action Steps**		**Action Steps**		**Action Steps**		**Action Steps**	
Research different business models (franchise, direct sales, start my own from scratch) including compensation plan and terms and conditions.		Secure domain and create website		Research different marketing platforms		Build email list			
Research start up and ongoing budget required for each business model		Who is my target market?		What countries or time zones do I want to market?		Follow up on inquiries			
Decide business model best suited for me		Create social media pages (Facebook, Instagram, LinkedIn, Pinterest)		Who is my niche audience?		Ask for the sale!			
Raise capital to start		Create content (one month in advance at a time) and schedule to post.		Place my first (and subsequent) advertisements					
Register Business Name		Gain followers							
Get started – Register with existing company		Start blog post							
Go through set up steps with company		Follow influencers in my niche							
Speak with accountant re: any other requirements to establish business		Create interest in my product and business							
Notes:		Notes:		Notes:		Notes:		Notes:	

WHAT THEY THINK IS NOT MY BUSINESS

You can see there are five milestones that, when completed, are equal to the big goal. These milestones are then broken down into actionable steps. The Action Planner isn't fully completed but you get the idea of how to fill it out. The big scary goal doesn't seem so scary when you're thinking of completing one action step at a time. Simply tick off each step as you go!

You can break each action step down further, if needed. For example, in the action step of raising capital to start your business, you may have individual ideas to accomplish such as: apply for a bank loan, increase a credit card limit, set up a savings plan, sell something, ask someone for a loan, get a job temporarily to increase your start up budget, etc. You could use a blank planner to break each step down more.

The more you can break down the milestones, the better. *Tip:* Avoid paralysis by analysis! It will be really easy to do nothing because you are considering and scrutinising every action required. That's defeating the purpose. Your action plan will re-shape along the way, so don't get too carried away with creating your steps. It is essential to write down your plan, but remain fluid. Most certainly, it will not go exactly to plan, so remain open to change along the way. Remember, until real-world action is taken, your goal will just remain a vision that you once had - even with a plan in place! Brainstorm the steps required to achieve what you want, and get into action as quickly as you can.

EFFECTIVE KICKASS ACTION

Example 2. Lose 10 kilograms

My Big Goal	My goal is to lose 10kg
My Why:	I want to feel fit and healthy, and be able to run 5km non-stop. Being 10kg lighter will give me the energy and confidence to be my best self and be a model of health to my kids, my partner and my friends.

Milestones

Milestones	Deadline
1. Determine a workout routine	
2. Create healthy eating behaviours	
3. Establish method of accountability	
4. Drop a dress size	
5. Complete the community 5km fun run	

Milestones

1. Determine workout routine	✓	2. Healthy eating behaviours	✓	3. Establish accountability	✓	4. Drop a dress size	✓	5. Complete 5km fun run	✓
Action Steps		Action Steps		Action Steps		Action Steps		Action Steps	
Research the local gyms		Research calorie controlled plans (WW, Lite n Easy etc)		Recruit a training buddy					
Decide and join a gym		Look into seeing a nutritionist		Hire a PT to be accountable to					
Book with a trainer to get started at the gym		Eat 2 pieces of fruit a day		Take my beginning measurements and weight					
Ask a friend to join me		Drink at least 1.5L of water a day		Track my eating and exercise behaviours on an app					
Schedule into my routine min 3 x per week exercise sessions at the gym		Reduce portion sizes							
Take the stairs at work		Eat 3 meals and 2 snacks max per day							
Walk at my lunch break 3x per week minimum									
Research yoga studios near home									
Notes:		Notes:		Notes:		Notes:		Notes:	

"If you spend too much time thinking about a thing, you'll never get it done."
~ Bruce Lee

ACTION

Using the Action Planner in Appendix II, break your goals down into milestones and actionable steps. Completing this Planner shouldn't take more than an hour at the absolute most. You will find that you will add to your planner as your journey goes on.

Set Your Time Frame

By breaking it down into timely milestones, the big end goal doesn't seem so overwhelming, does it? At this point, you may be starting to feel excited, for you can see how you're going to create this great life you desire. Or conversely, you could be feeling a little anxious as you can now see what is required to make it a reality. Either way, you've totally got this! The fact you now know what you need to do makes you miles ahead of 90% of people who give up before they even began.

The final step in creating your plan is putting a deadline on each step. You will see in the top section of the Action Planner, to the right of the milestone, a space for the date you will complete each milestone. This is to ensure accountability to take the action by a certain time. I would recommend also putting a deadline on each action step to make sure action continues to be steadily taken. Again, work backwards. For example, if your goal is to lose 10 kilograms in eight months, when will you have established an exercise routine? When will you be able to run 4 kilometres non-stop? Put a date beside each milestone, and each individual step.

It's important to remember to **set your goal in concrete, and the timeline in sand.** Most people *overestimate* what is possible in the short term, and *underestimate* what is possible in the long term. Allow yourself to absolutely dream big however, know you will hit snags along the way that could push back your timeline, or steps that may take longer than anticipated. This is where we draw on our arsenal of tools to keep our vibration up, and our momentum going. The timeline is there as a guide, and something to work towards, but be fluid in the date. For example, if it takes you 12 months, instead of eight, to lose those 10 kilograms, does that really matter in the grand scheme of things? Not at all, because the person you will be at 10 kilograms lighter is worth that extra time getting there!

Plan for Course Changes

Very rarely will things go according to plan. You have your arsenal of tools to draw on when you hit a rough patch, and you most certainly will face more than one or two along the way. Expect it, and plan for it. You may need to change course, change tactics, or you may even find your ultimate end goal shift.

Wherever your journey takes you, is the right direction for you. As one opportunity opens, embrace it and trust the process. Be firm in moving forward toward your ultimate life, be fluid in how you get there, and your time line. You may even find yourself way off track to where you want to go, and that's ok. Just simply course correct and keep moving forward. There will be challenges, people and circumstances that will try to take you out of the game. But remain decided on your path and keep moving forward, your way.

> "Success seems to be connected with action. Successful people keep moving. They make mistakes, but they don't quit."
> **~ Conrad Hilton**

Whatever life throws at you, think of it as a test from The Universe. How badly do you want the new job? A successful business? To meet the love of your life? Be in the best shape of your life? Be prepared to be tested, and commit to overcoming anything that is put in your way. You can spend time working on what YOU want and how you want to live every day, or you can spend your time dealing with a life you're not happy with. The choice is yours. Will you 'feel' like taking the next step when you hit a difficult time? Probably not, but it is this moment that will divide the weak from the strong, the undecided from the decided and the uncommitted from the committed.

Start as You Mean to Go On

How you start your journey to what you want is an indication of how you plan to go on. Are you starting this journey half-heartedly, or are you fully committed to seeing it through to the end? The same goes for how you start your day. Do you drag yourself out of bed, after snoozing the alarm clock five times, feeling cranky and

EFFECTIVE KICKASS ACTION

just wanting to curl back under the covers? Or do you bound out of bed, excited to get the day started, with determination and commitment to taking serious action?

As you start, so you will go on. I've never really been an early morning person by choice but over the years, I have developed a habit of getting up at 5 am. I love the peacefulness of the early hours of the morning and the opportunity to set the tone for my day, my way. It is when I have the most clarity and, surprisingly the most energy.

Sure, I've had days where I've slept in, only to be completely rushing the girls off to school, not making my bed, and I've found the rest of my day to flow in a similar pattern - chaotic, rushed and pressed for time. On those days, I certainly am not productive and do not feel satisfied with what I've actioned by the end of the day. When I start my day at 5 am, by the time my girls have woken up, I've had two hours of aligning with my goals, getting my mindset right, taking action in my business and preparing myself for a truly fabulous day.

Develop a morning ritual that works for you. Perhaps you're more of a night owl, rather than an early riser. The point is to create a habit of setting yourself up for a productive day. When are you most productive? When do you work best? It is about giving yourself the best possible chance of success. For me, I am definitely not as productive in the evening as I am in the early morning. Do I love getting up at 5 am? I wouldn't say yes, and it was certainly not something I found easy to do in the beginning. However, what I do love is how much I get done first thing in the morning, and how much closer to my goals I am.

ACTION

When are you most productive in your day? Have a look at your schedule and plan when you are going to work on your goal. Make it a priority and carve time out to take the action needed.

"Action trumps indecision every single time."
~ Ana McRae

It's Action Time!

It's game day baby. You have everything you need to create the life your heart truly desires. Now it's time to put pedal to the metal; to put your money where your mouth is. As I say to my girls, "I wish I could do it for you, but I can't." This is where you take the reins and take off. This is your time.

Develop your plan of action, then work your plan. You are responsible for where you are now, and where you are going. You can absolutely have everything you want, by DOING what it takes to get there. If you can think it, you can absolutely have it. The disconnect is what action you are willing to take, to get you there. No action, no change. Action taken consistently and intentionally will change your life.

EFFECTIVE KICKASS ACTION

"The future depends on what you do today."
~ Mahatma Gandhi

You absolutely deserve to live your best life possible, regardless of what other people think. I truly believe in you. This is where you take over and begin to create everything you want. To say I'm excited for you is an understatement. Take your life to the next level. Starting today. What are you waiting for?

CHAPTER SUMMARY

- Real world action is required to create the life you desire.

- Being consistent in taking action towards your goals will almost certainly guarantee your success.

- Work backwards and break your big goal down into smaller milestones, then further into actionable steps, makes it less scary and overwhelming.

- Give yourself a deadline to achieve each step and milestone! Plan, but more importantly, start taking action!

- You and only you can make your dreams become a reality.

"Be the hero of your own movie."
~ Joe Rogan

Afterword

A journalist was curious about human characteristics and how different paths are taken in life, creating different circumstances and outcomes. In the pursuit of understanding any differences that may exist, the journalist hit the streets to find out.

She decided to interview a homeless man to learn about his life path, decisions and actions taken that led him to where he was today. After some reluctance and trepidation, he opened up describing his traumatic childhood. He explained how his father was an alcoholic, how he and his brother suffered abuse and trauma throughout their younger years, and how his father had gambled all of their money away, losing the family home. He talked about the lack of opportunities he had in his life because of his circumstances and how the streets were his only answer. "How could I end up in any other situation other than homeless, given my father was an alcoholic, we lost everything and I was abused as a kid?"

The journalist left heartbroken, wondering if it was a matter of chance, the parents and family you were born into, or the opportunities and circumstances presented to you, that would determine your life path?

WHAT THEY THINK IS NOT MY BUSINESS

She decided she wanted to hear from a highly successful person to uncover how they had reached the level they had, and if the dice had in fact rolled their way from the moment they were born.

After many phone calls and emails, the journalist secured an appointment to speak with the city's most successful Chief Executive Officer. The interview was very detailed as he outlined his path from starting out at the front desk greeting guests, to now being the CEO of the city's largest bank. While his resume was impressive, what the journalist really wanted to know about was his upbringing. The CEO hesitated. *What has he got to hide*, thought the journalist. The CEO did not usually talk about his childhood, but in this instance he was willing to share. He explained how his father was an alcoholic, how he and his brother had experienced abuse and trauma throughout their childhood and how his father had gambled all their money away, losing their family home. He talked about how being thrown onto the streets had minimised the lack of opportunities that came his way.

When asked how he had overcome such traumatic beginnings to create such phenomenal results in his life, he replied, "How could I end up in any other situation other than successful, given my father was an alcoholic, we lost everything and I was abused as a kid?"

This parable demonstrates that no matter where you have come from, no matter where you are starting from, you and only you decide the path you will take. The power resides in the individual person to create their life. Use your circumstances to fuel you to go exactly where you want.

The time is now to go live your life, your way.

Resources

Personal Development Market Size, Share & Trends Analysis Report (2020). Grand View Research. Accessed 21 April 2021, https://www.grandviewresearch.com/industry-analysis/personal-development-market.

Jung, C. (1952). *Synchronicity: An Acausal Connecting Principle.* Princeton, NJ. Princeton University Press.

Mailer, J. (2000-2004). *Personal Development Program.* National College of Business. QLD, Australia.

Maroutian, E. (2015). *Thirty: A Collection of Personal Quotes, Advice, and Lessons.* United States: Createspace Independent Publishing Platform.

Sinek, S, Docker, P & Mead, D. (2017). *Find Your Why.* London, UK: Penguin Books Ltd.

About the Author

Jaime Laing is a self-made powerhouse having overcome the struggles of being raised in a single parent family, with little money, to become a successful entrepreneur and mum. Raised in Western Sydney, Australia during the 80s, Jaime fought the stigma of coming from a home without a dad, being different from her peers and desperately looked for acceptance and approval from everyone she encountered.

Jaime's own journey of self-discovery and personal development has led her to assist individuals globally in reaching their full potential and to create the life of their dreams.

Jaime has aimed high in everything she has done from completing a Bachelor of Applied Science (Exercise and Sport Science), Certificate in Life Coaching, and is the only woman in the world to hold a 5th Degree Black Belt in Hapkido Moohakkwan. She built a multiple six-figure traditional business from scratch with her husband Kevin, and is an Online Business Coach and Entrepreneur.

ABOUT THE AUTHOR

Jaime's work and passion lies in coaching and mentoring others to live their absolute best life, despite what other people think. She has trained individuals across the globe and it gives her no greater joy than to see people achieve greatness in their own lives, and accomplish more than they thought was possible.

Jaime lives on the Central Coast, NSW, Australia with her husband Kevin, their two beautiful daughters, Brooklyn and Indiana and their boxer, Willow.

Connect with Jaime:
www.jaimelaing.com
Email: jaime@thenextlevelfreedom.com
Facebook: www.facebook.com/thenextlevelfreedom
Instagram: www.instagram.com/next.level.freedom

Acknowledgements

I am a strong woman because a strong woman raised me. I wouldn't have become the woman I am without the unconditional love and support of my mum, Trish. I will never be able to thank you enough for everything you have done and continue to do for me. Thank you, Mum.

To my big sister Lisa. While we joke about who is the smarter one between us, I couldn't have completed this without your help. I looked up to you when I was baby and I still do to this day. Thank you, Issy.

To my husband Kevin. This book would not have happened if you had not planted that seed in my head over 15 years ago. You have been my pillar of strength and have given me the confidence to know I can do anything, and with you by my side, I know that's true. Thank you for your unwavering belief and support. I couldn't do this crazy life without you.

To my angels Brooklyn and Indiana. Thank you for choosing me as your mum. I wanted to write this book for you both, as a demonstration of striving for your goals and achieving more than you could have imagined. During moments where I have felt challenged, your words of encouragement have amazed me and driven me to continue on. I love you both more than words can explain, and I'm forever grateful for you both.

WHAT THEY THINK IS NOT MY BUSINESS

A special mention to my step-dad James. You have shown me what it means to have a father's unconditional love and for that I am forever grateful. Thank you for being the father I have always wanted.

My thanks also to my friends, colleagues, past clients, and team members for taking the time, without hesitation, in writing your heartfelt words in your testimonials: Alison, Borland, Dabs, Fran, Johanna, Kazza, Kirsty, Lise, Nicola, Sandy and Sherie.

To my mentor, colleague and friend Kirsty. I will never forget your belief in me when I couldn't see it in myself. Thank you for coming into my life and giving me the space to step into my own greatness, whilst holding the bar high for me to reach. I aspire to make you proud and look forward to being on that stage with you celebrating many more milestones to come.

Finally, to the person who inspired me and showed me that anything was possible, if you believed. Thank you Jon. My life is better because I met you.

Testimonials

"I have had the pleasure of knowing and becoming close friends with Jaime Laing over the past 20 years. Throughout this time, I've seen her growth, professionalism and self development blossom from managing a fitness gym, personal training, group exercise instructing, life coaching, becoming a mother to her two beautiful girls (her proudest achievement without a doubt) to taking a huge leap of faith creating from scratch a successful martial arts business with her husband.

What stands out the most to me about Jaime, both personally and from a business stand point, along with her journey through all the different stages of her life, is witnessing first hand her drive, determination, perseverance and belief within herself. She continually applies different tools of motivation and self development to improve herself in all aspects of her life, with the balance of work/family time the utmost of importance, along with continuing her pursuit to be the best version of herself she can be!

Jaime went outside the box in 2018 to start an online business and as her good friend, I believe she has found her calling! From an experienced manager, business woman and now an online personal development entrepreneur, her journey continues to evolve.

Jaime is a go-getter, chase your dreams, live your best life kind of woman who will succeed in anything she puts her mind to and I'm thankful to call her my mate."

~ Sandy Furner,
WMC Welterweight Australian Muay Thai Boxing Champion

WHAT THEY THINK IS NOT MY BUSINESS

"Jaime has been my mentor for the last eight months. She has brought a level of depth, empowerment and support to every conversation we have had. Her commitment to enrich her life and others is an inspiration. She creates a safe place to be vulnerable and show up authentically as one's best version. I feel very fortunate to have crossed paths with Jaime not only for all her guidance on identifying limiting beliefs but also to have her be an example of the mentor I want to become."

~ **Johanna Aguirre, Lead Your Path**

"I met Jaime 20 years ago and she has been an amazing inspiration in not only my life but many others. She brings the best out in everyone she touches. From her own learnings and experiences, Jaime helps you to achieve the life you believe you should have.

Negative self doubt was a part of my life and after 6 months of Life Coaching with Jaime, I started ticking off goals, and the more I did the more I believed in myself. From coaching with Jaime, I achieved so many firsts: I bought a car, I bought a home, and I travelled overseas. Things I never believed I could do. The one thing that I could never have done, without growing myself, was selling my home in Sydney and moving to Perth to be with my son, daughter-in-law and grandchildren.

Jaime is the most inspirational person in my world."

~ **Tracey Borland**

TESTIMONIALS

"I have worked alongside Jaime now for the last couple of years and have seen her grow as a student, as a business owner, and as a leader. Her commitment to her own personal growth is exemplary. Jaime continues to step up as a leader in our business community demonstrating her strengths to assist and mentor others in a meaningful way. It has been a joy to get to know Jaime and see her transform into the passionate business owner she is today."

~ Lise Reitsma, Your Dream Lifestyle

"Personal trainer to lifelong friend. I met Jaime over 11 years ago through my boyfriend (now husband) who worked with Jaime's hubby, Kev. I started Personal Training with Jaime to get into shape for my wedding and I expected that she would go easy on me, as we were friends. I was wrong. I got great results and our "training/therapy sessions" helped me remain calm and look amazing on my wedding day. Our friendship has deepened and strengthened over the years, and our kids' friendship also continues to grow.

Jaime is an amazing friend, trainer, mentor and incredible business woman. I am constantly blown away by her amazing positive attitude and her ability to face any obstacles and soar over them. Jaime started as a work colleague's wife, became a friend, a Personal Trainer and then a best friend. My life is blessed with Jaime as my friend."

~ Sarah "Dabs" Dabinett-Hutchins

WHAT THEY THINK IS NOT MY BUSINESS

"I've known Jaime for over 13 years where we met at the gym where she instructed. I remember that I always looked forward to her classes, she worked us hard in every class and encouraged us to push ourselves that little bit more each time. I learnt from her then to push myself a little more than the last class I attended, to challenge my personal best.

Jaime has helped me to work through barriers that I have, the lack of self-confidence in certain areas like anything to do with an audience. She is so patient and understanding with me when I have the most embarrassing uncontrollable nerves that strike me when I'm out of my comfort zone.

Jaime has a beautiful friendly way about her which allows me to feel comfortable to speak openly while she listens intently whether that is with life or business. Jaime has helped me to recognise and focus on the lessons to take away from the challenging times in life and in business that emotions can distract you from and provides guidance to work through the challenges so I can become the best version of myself."

~ Francesca Surace, Awakened Ambition

BE COACHED & MENTORED BY JAIME DIRECTLY!

Jaime has a passion for helping others take their life to the next level and works directly with like-minded, driven individuals. Those who are serious and hungry to create success on their terms. Those who are seeking to:

- Work a flexible schedule
- Create success and financial freedom
- Build a global online business
- Help others create success
- Control their earning potential
- Be part of a booming industry - Personal Development!

Be coached and mentored directly by Jaime, in a proven business model, with an award winning product line. Mention you have read this book and receive a BONUS goal setting mentoring session for anyone who moves forward and works directly with her.

To learn more about whom Jaime partners with and how you can work directly with her, go to the link below or scan the QR code for obligation-free information.

www.jaimelaing.com

FREE BONUS
MIND POWER BOOT CAMP ONLINE PROGRAM

Enjoy the unparalleled freedom that comes when you take control of your most powerful asset - Your Mind.

What to expect from the FREE Mind Power Boot Camp:

- Maximise your personal power
- Eliminate negative thinking
- Implement powerful techniques and principles
- Discover your passion and purpose
- Increase your earning capacity
- Strengthen your intuition
- Increase your health and vitality
- Gain greater access to solutions to your problems

Instant Access

Simply go to the link below or scan the QR code to register and gain instant access to your FREE Mind Power Boot Camp:

https://www.jaimelaing.com/MindPowerBootCamp

7 STEPS TO ABUNDANCE
BREAK THROUGH THE WEALTH BARRIER

An intensive 12 day online program designed to get you on purpose to your financial goals, educate you on the strategies and mindset around wealth creation, and strip away the counterproductive ways of thinking, using and handling money.

This online program will teach you how to take control of your financial circumstances, and dramatically shift your reality.

Course includes topics:
- Karma & Understanding the Energy Around Money
- Money Knowledge & Basic Set Up
- Develop Your Wealth Super Powers

12 days of content designed for daily home study with applicable exercises to implement immediately in your life and start your journey of 7 Steps to Abundance.

Simply go to the link below or scan the QR code and get ready for incredible shifts over 12 Days:

https://www.jaimelaing.com/7Steps-to-Abundance

Jaime Laing

WHAT THEY THINK IS NOT MY BUSINESS

NEXT LEVEL FREEDOM
YOUR LIFE. YOUR WAY.

is a leadership specialist who understands what it takes to create success and live an ideal life. Growing up in a single-parent home in Western Sydney taught Jaime the value of hard work and perseverance. She was determined not to live a life of scarcity and mediocrity and her dedication to this led to her becoming an entrepreneur in her early 20s. Her achievements include building a multiple six-figure business from scratch and becoming the world's highest ranked female Black Belt in Hapkido Moohakkwan. Jaime's passion lies in assisting others overcome self-limiting beliefs, enabling them to achieve greatness in their own lives and accomplish more than they could imagine. Jaime knows success is a journey and not simply a destination, and this perspective has helped her inspire, mentor and develop hundreds of individuals globally in the health and fitness, sales, marketing and business sectors. In her book What Other People Think Is Not My Business, Jaime shares strategies and leaderships skills that she has used to create success and that you can easily implement into your life to achieve your dreams.

Overcoming What Other People Think & The Fear of Judgement

- Releasing fear around other's opinions
- Owning your past, your present and your future
- Going for what you want despite what other people say

You Get To Choose Your Life

- Removing the blinkers and seeing the limitless potential
- Releasing the past to create the future
- Focusing on what you desire and being open to opportunities

Being Your Greatest Advocate & Doing What It Takes

- Mastering your mind to out create any situation
- Detaching from the outcome and keeping your vision strong
- Learning how to finish as strong as you start

 +61 421 862 225   www.jaimelaing.com   jaime@thenextlevelfreedom.com

WHAT THEY THINK IS NOT MY BUSINESS

NOTES

www.ingramcontent.com/pod-product-compliance
Lightning Source LLC
Chambersburg PA
CBHW021146080526
44588CB00008B/236